21.84

GP

LIBERTIES WITH LIBERTY

Liberties with Liberty

The Fascinating History
of America's Proudest Symbol

Nancy Jo Fox

E. P. DUTTON   NEW YORK
In association with the
MUSEUM OF AMERICAN FOLK ART   NEW YORK

Photograph of the Statue of Liberty by Jake
Rajs on page ii © 1985 N.Y.

Photograph of the head of the Statue of Liberty
by Jake Rajs on page iii © 1983 N.Y.

Book design by Marilyn Rey

First published, 1986, in the United States by E. P. Dutton. / All rights reserved under International and
Pan-American Copyright Conventions. / No part of this book may be reproduced or transmitted in any form or
by any means, electronic or mechanical, including photocopy, recording, or any storage and retrieval system
now known or to be invented, without permission in writing from the publishers, except by a reviewer who
wishes to quote brief passages in connection with a review written for inclusion in a magazine, newspaper, or
broadcast. / Published simultaneously in Canada by Fitzhenry & Whiteside Limited, Toronto. / W / Published
in the United States by E.P. Dutton, a division of New American Library, 2 Park Avenue, New York, N.Y. 10016.
/ Printed and bound by Dai Nippon Printing Co., Ltd., Tokyo, Japan. / Library of Congress Catalog Card
Number: 85-70848. / ISBN: 0-525-24377-1 (cloth); ISBN: 0-525-48192-3 (DP).
10 9 8 7 6 5 4 3 2 1 First Edition

Dedicated to my parents who gave me
the greatest liberty of all — the
freedom to be myself.

Celebrations have always been an integral part of American life. They rekindle our spirit, reawaken our patriotic fervor, and reaffirm our faith in basic democratic values. Because celebrations ignite these feelings of pride and patriotism, it is important that we provide an opportunity for as many Americans as possible to participate in them.

Xerox Corporation is particularly pleased to sponsor "Liberties with Liberty" and to encourage widespread participation by others. Over the years, Liberty has become the single most important manifestation of this nation's faith in democratic principles and ideals. Liberty has helped us recall the ideals of our past and reinforced the responsibility these ideals place on all Americans. Liberty is very simply the national symbol of our determination to remain free.

But Liberty itself is not free. Thomas Jefferson taught us that "eternal vigilance is the price of liberty." It is our hope that this exhibition and book help in that process of "eternal vigilance." As a corporate institution that has gained much from our free society, we recognize our dependence on Liberty for our very existence and we are proud to help demonstrate the inestimable value all Americans place on their liberty.

David T. Kearns
Chairman & Chief Executive Officer
Xerox Corporation

LIBERTIES WITH LIBERTY

INTRODUCTION

The New Colossus

Not like the brazen giant of Greek fame,
With conquering limbs astride from land to land;
Here at our sea-washed, sunset gates shall stand
A mighty woman with a torch whose flame
Is the imprisoned lightning, and her name
Mother of Exiles. From her beacon-hand
Glows world-wide welcome; her mild eyes command
The air-bridged harbor that twin cities frame.
"Keep, ancient lands, your storied pomp!" cries she
With silent lips. "Give me your tired, your poor,
Your huddled masses yearning to breathe free.
The wretched refuse of your teeming shore.
Send these, the homeless, tempest-tossed to me,
I lift my lamp beside the golden door!"

Emma Lazarus[1]

Almost every American schoolchild used to learn this poem, particularly the last five lines, which are now enshrined in the American vernacular along with the Fourth of July, Mom's apple pie, baseball, the Stars and Stripes, and, of course, the Statue of Liberty itself.

The Statue of Liberty was 100 years old on July 4, 1984. The gift of France to the American people, she was designed by the Alsatian sculptor, Frederick Auguste Bartholdi, who used his mother's face as his model; and was assembled piece by piece in the studio of Gaget, Gautheier et Cie until she rose high above the rooftops of Paris.[2] Although Bartholdi acknowledged the Colossus of Rhodes as his main inspiration, Liberty's iconography is a revamping of stock themes: the reincarnation of faith, truth, and liberty. In the lavishly illustrated 1766 edition of Cesare Ripa's *Iconologia*, the great Renaissance iconographic compendium originally published in 1593, Faith appears helmeted, a classical female dressed in white, cradling an open book of the New Testament and the tablets of the Old Testament.[3] Her right hand is raised, holding a flaming candle shaped like a heart, symbol of the illuminating power of faith to dispel ignorance and superstition. Truth stands with a foot on the globe, one hand bearing a palm branch and the other touching the sun and its rays.[4] Liberty's crown, too, is a familiar image from the past, especially common in religious art from all over the world, the nimbus or radiating crown relating to the sun and its rays to the seven known planets. By the third century B.C. when the Roman Republic built her a temple on the Aventine Hill,[5] the Goddess of Liberty appeared in art as a robed female holding a scepter, indicating sovereignty over herself, with a liberty-loving cat at her feet alongside a broken jug (shattered symbol of confinement) and crowned by the Phrygian cap, the *pilleus libertatis*, bestowed upon slaves when granted freedom.[6]

The Statue of Liberty arrived in America on June 17, 1886, and was officially installed on a star-shaped base designed by an American, Richard Morris Hunt, at Bedloe's Island in New York harbor, where it was dedicated by President Grover Cleveland on October 28, 1886. There she has remained, a beacon of hope and *the* symbol of freedom to Americans and to the rest of the world.

Too unwieldy to be shipped to America in one

—for the statue weighs 225 tons and stands 151 feet high—this copper-skinned, iron-skeletoned "wonder woman" was shipped via Rouen in 210 wooden crates to be reassembled here. But that was not her first visit to the United States.[7] Miss Liberty's right arm with its torch captured the imagination of Americans long before the entire statue was completed. In 1876 the right arm was brought to the United States for the Centennial Exposition at Philadelphia, remaining on display until 1877, when it was moved to Madison Square in New York City.[8] Viewed by thousands until 1884, the arm was then shipped back to France to be assembled with the rest of the statue.[9] The three hundred sections of the "Mother of Exiles" was held together by 300,000 rivets and supported by a marvel of iron engineering created by Alexandre Gustave Eiffel—his only structure in the United States—famous for another symbol of another city and country, the Eiffel Tower in Paris.[10]

The Statue of Liberty, originally titled "Liberty Enlightening the World," will always be a magnificent sight. But this extraordinary symbol of American freedom, wearing a crown of rays, holding in one hand a book inscribed with the date of the Declaration of Independence while the other lifts a large flaming torch, did not always have this form.

Whether stray Vikings, St. Brendan, Christopher Columbus, or Amerigo Vespucci discovered the New World, the promise of great wealth, strange virgin lands, religious freedom, or the thrill of adventure appealed to many who wished to better their lives even while risking great danger. Danger came from the native Indians who, while enemies of the Colonists, were viewed by the white man as exotic symbols not only of the new continent but also of the unrestricted, natural life that Europeans could find in this new country. Just as females had come to symbolize the other major continents—Asia, Africa, and Europe—it was the American Indian Queen who first personified the New World.

With the publication of Martin Waldseemüller's *Cosmographiae Introductio* in 1507, the entire western New World became known as "America."[11] From 1570 to 1765, America was allegorized in the arts by the Indian Queen, with the attributes of a Caribbean culture.[12] After 1759, America came to be understood as England's thirteen Atlantic seaboard Colonies, an image reinforced by a growing realization, here and abroad, of the importance of these Colonies as a force affecting English domestic policies, its imperial policy, and the international power struggle, as well as a growing desire in the Colonies for a distinctive national identity. A fresh symbol was needed by 1765 to satisfy these strong nationalistic longings. So, from 1765 to 1783, the Indian Princess—a daughter of Britannia but a rebellious child—came to represent the thirteen Colonies, as distinct from the "continent" America.[13] After 1783, when the term *America* signified the independent United States, the Indian Princess continued as its symbol until about 1815,[14] gradually metamorphosing into a Plumed Greek Goddess.[15] By the early nineteenth century, the Indian Princess and Greek Goddess were joined by Brother or Cousin Jonathan, Uncle Sam, the Goddess of Liberty, Columbia, and, finally, the Statue of Liberty.

The Indian Queen that was universally used by the end of the sixteenth century personified America as the Western Hemisphere. She appeared on maps of early explorers and in European atlases, in book illustrations and in political prints, as well as in ceramics, paintings, and sculptures.[16] This formidable, bare-breasted, barefoot woman usually wore a feathered headdress, skirt, cape, and jeweled anklets.[17] In the earliest representations, a club was her weapon; later, she carried a bow and arrows.[18] The armadillo and llama are shown at her feet or as her mount, later replaced by an alligator.[19] The engraving by Adrien Collaert II after Marten de Vos's design *Personification of America* (fig. 1) shows the immediate popularity of this image. A parrot, then indigenous to the Carolinas, is perched on a branch and, monkeys, a puma, and a stag accompany her, amid tropical foliage.[20] The natural wealth of the New World—a constant lure to adventurers—was shown in the form of ingots, vessels of gold, chests laden with jewelry, and the European motif of cornucopias spilling forth fruit and flowers. A savage touch was the severed head of a man pierced by an arrow, lying near her feet.[21]

By 1603, as her iconography became standardized, the Indian Queen appeared on newspaper mastheads, coins, and cartouches. She continued to be seen in a succession of emblem books and dictionaries, from the first illustrated edition of Cesare Ripa's *Iconologia* in 1603 to a *Collection of Emblematical Figures*, published in London in 1779, as well as in Thomas Sheraton's *Cabinet Dictionary*, published in London in 1803, which greatly influenced the design of American furniture and decorative arts.[22]

The American Indian brave, fascinating enemy, enjoyed a brief appearance on Colonial seals, mastheads, weathervanes, and state seals—and, of course, as the disguise for the Sons of Liberty in the Boston Tea Party of 1774—but the female Indian symbol dominated.[23]

1. Adrien Collaert II after Marten de Vos: *Personification of America*. Europe. 1765–1775. Engraving, 8⅜″ x 10⅜″. The Indian Queen, symbol of the fourth continent, was a swarthy Amazon dressed in feathers, armed with a bow and arrows and a tomahawk. An armadillo, llama, or alligator appeared at her side or as her mount, as seen here, where against an expansive wilderness she watches Indians during a hunt and in battle. (The Henry Francis du Pont Winterthur Museum, Winterthur, Delaware)

2. Thomas Colley: *The Reconciliation Between Britannia and Her Daughter America*. London. 1782. Colored engraving, 8¹/₁₆″ x 12⅞″. English and American cartoons depicted every nuance of affection, alienation, matricide, and reconciliation in the mother–daughter relationship between England and the Colonies. During the peace talks of 1782 and 1783, mother and daughter are reconciled as Britain requests a "buss," slang at that time for a kiss. (Print Collection, The New York Public Library: Astor, Lenox and Tilden Foundations, New York City)

The Indian Princess of the American Colonies, emerging in the 1760s, differed from her rich, voluptuous mother. Although still swarthy with long, dark hair, she no longer appeared to belong to an alien race but rather to be a distant cousin of Britannia still in feathers, but sometimes in a long, flowing gown.[24] This youthful, haughty version was less savage and less Caribbean than the Indian Queen of the Western Hemisphere. The bow and arrows, never the club, was her weapon, although the severed head had disappeared. Gone, too, were the monkeys, the llama, and the armadillo.[25] The alligator and palm trees remained, for they are native to Georgia and Florida, but the Indian Princess was more often seen with a rattlesnake helping to defend her from attack.[26] Found only on this continent, the rattlesnake was considered a deadly, fascinating reptile in Europe and so became one of the earliest native symbols to accompany the female image. As the rattlesnake has no eyelids, it came to signify constant vigilance. As it never attacks without provocation and never surrenders to an aggressor, it became a powerful symbol of the rebellious Colonists, accompanied by the slogan *Don't Tread on Me* before and during the Revolutionary War.[27] In a cartoon of the period, an angry Britannia threatens America with her upraised spear and grasps one of the feathers in America's skirt while a fierce rattlesnake defends the Princess.[28]

Signs of the natural wealth of the Caribbean, Peru, and Mexico—chests of gold, jewelry, or the cornucopia—were replaced by the cargo ships and bales of tobacco and cotton representing Colonial trade.[29] And now, beneath the feet of the Indian Princess appeared the symbols of monarchy—the lions, crowns, and chains of England, as well as the key to the French Bastille.[30] She would evolve into the *idée fixe* of the attainment of freedom, pictured with the Goddess of Liberty and reaching for the goddess's cap and pole.[31] This feathered Indian Princess was still armed with the bow and arrows, tomahawk, or scalping knife, but has begun to brandish a sword, a spear or a peace pipe, and may even wear sandals.[32]

The American flag officially adopted by the Continental Congress in 1776 incorporated the Indian Princess, as did the Shield with thirteen stars and stripes.[33] In the popular media, she was used to illustrate America's daughter–mother relationship to Britain. Wonderful English and American cartoons illustrate every nuance of affection, alienation, conflict, and reconciliation in this relationship. During the peace talks of 1782–1783, an English cartoon depicts mother and daughter making up, as Britannia calls out, "Be a good girl and give me a Buss," and America replies, "Dear Mama, say no more about it" (fig. 2).[34]

Another early native symbol representing the young American government was the pine tree, appearing on the shilling issued in Massachusetts in 1652.[35] The pine tree is related to one of the universal ideas, the tree of life, ever green, ever bearing. This tree motif continued to the Revolutionary War when it became the Liberty Tree. Shown as a tall, spreading shade tree, it was used by the Sons of Liberty, a secret patriotic society begun before the Revolutionary War, as a gathering place for meetings and where they hanged British officials in effigy. The Liberty Tree appeared in drawings, on printed fabrics, and seals, and as recently as 1976, on the United States thirteen-cent stamp. Liberty Poles, representing Liberty Trees, were erected in town squares throughout the thirteen Colonies and were often topped with Liberty Caps.[36]

The Liberty Cap stems from 750 B.C., when, as liberated slaves, the people of Troy and the Phrygians of Asia Minor wore the Roman *pilleus*, a felt cap, as a symbol of personal liberty and national independence.[37] Its antecedents include the cap of Athena, patroness of Athens, seen in Roman representations, as well as those worn by King Midas, the Amazons, Mithras, and other early figures associated with the Near East.[38] The cap was joined to the pole as a symbol of freedom when Salturnius conquered Rome in 263 B.C. where, in a burst of inspiration, he raised the cap on a pikestaff to show that the slaves who joined his fight would be freed.[39] In the third century, B.C., caps were carried aloft on spears during festivals.[40]

The French, also staking out territory in the New World, sympathized with the American fight against their old enemy, the British, and aided the revolutionary struggle. It was natural that the red Liberty Cap of the French Revolution of 1789, the *bonnet rouge*, a closer cousin of *pilleus libertatis*, become an important accessory of various American representations, including the Indian Princess, Goddess of Liberty, Columbia, and Liberty. It appeared on the heads of these figures and was carried on a Liberty Pole or on a flagpole in engravings, political cartoons, paintings, carvings, seals, and coins.[41] Often a carved cap was carried in patriotic parades or adorned wooden statues during this time of political unrest.[42]

After the Revolution, England was eager to maintain trade with her former Colonies, and the exchange of imports and exports was shown in cartoons by Mercury and bales of goods and cargo ships.[43] Soon the Indian Princess began to merge with the classical figure and to lose her symbolic meaning, appearing mostly in cartouches or engraved on stock certificates.[44] During the nineteenth century, mass production of Indian figures to adorn cigar stores further lessened the Princess's patriotic significance; and she continues to appear rather ignominiously to this day on labels for cigars and cigar boxes, sometimes joined by a classical figure.

Another classical inheritance familiar to most Americans is the Bald Eagle, which is not really bald but has a white feathered head. It appeared before 1782 when it was adopted as one element of the Great Seal of the United States.[45] In Roman times, the eagle had been the sign of power and majesty, the symbol of Jove, cared for by Hebe. With English recognition of the sovereignty of the United States, the Indian Princess, now Britain's "free sister," appeared carrying the flag, often topped with the Liberty Cap, but now was accompanied by the Bald Eagle and the beloved first president, George Washington. As she assumed her new role, her facial features were no longer those of an Indian. Her skin became lighter and her profile and hairstyle more classical. Now she rested by fluted columns and urns, bestowing olive and laurel wreaths on famous, honored Americans. She traveled in chariots, sometimes accompanied by a new set of sisters: the Goddess of Justice, holding the scales signifying exactness and rectitude, an attribute, of Aequitas, the Roman Goddess of Equity; the Goddess of Wisdom; and Liberty.[46] Her attire became that of the Greek Goddess of Liberty.

Although the Indian Princess appeared among classical motifs, she was clearly Indian when barefoot, scantily dressed in feathered skirt and headdress, and armed with a bow and arrows or a tomahawk. There was something real about the Indian female, oldest and most durable symbol. She lived in a particular part of the world; she was part of a historical race; she was present throughout three hundred years of colonization and conquests in the New World; she had personified the Western Hemisphere since mid-sixteenth century and America until mid-eighteenth century. Even in 1808, a set of engravings of the four continents shows America as the Indian Princess dressed in a feathered headdress and flanked by two tomahawks and guarded by a rattlesnake. The theme of the four continents that fascinated and delighted Europe as early as the sixteenth century continued in popularity during the late eighteenth and nineteenth centuries[47] (fig. 3).

Still, the classical trend persisted, and soon the Princess's headdress changed from eagle feathers to ostrich plumes worn in a turban, bonnet, or helmet.[48] The ostrich plumes maintained a certain continuity of outward tradition with the Princess while, in reality, expressing a radical change of spirit. By the late 1790s, it was not clear whether a feathered Indian Princess had changed into a Greek goddess or whether a Greek goddess had placed feathers or plumes in her hair. The feathers were soon replaced by a helmet or an olive or laurel wreath, and the bow and arrows by a spear and a shield. This new classical lady with flowing brown hair was tall, full breasted, and draped in a toga and cloak to her ankles, revealing her feet clad in sandals. The Plumed Goddess also held the caduceus, the staff of Mercury with two snakes intertwined around it.[49] In Greek mythology it was a herald's wand or staff, and with a pair of wings added, it became Hermes's wand.[50] The name for Hermes in ancient Rome was Mercury, and messengers carried his symbol as a sign of neutrality. Roman *medicos* searching battlefields for the wounded would carry the caduceus to establish their noncombatant status.[51] The young country, weary after its own Revolutionary War, wanted neutrality and peace with the rest of the world.

The artificially invented Plumed Greek Goddess possessed a certain theatrical quality, imagined by her neoclassical creators. English prints published between 1780 and 1815 show how frequently America, the fourth part of the world, was now interpreted as the United States of America and how readily the Plumed Goddess became its personification.[52] This American ideal, the genius of America, or as Thomas Jefferson referred to her, "a fine female figure," appeared on an amazing variety of artifacts and art in the 1780s, as the discoveries at Pompeii spurred a neoclassical revival steeping the young nation in an awareness of the wonders of ancient Greece and Rome.[53] This revival was reflected in the oratory of the day and in academic interest in the gods, goddesses, and legends of classical times, fueling a desire for a modern re-creation of the democracy of ancient Greece and a new Roman Republic. Architecture and furniture, as well as the decorative and folk arts, showed powerful classical influences in this American Federal period, comparable to the Empire and Directoire eras of Europe.

In 1791 an oval watercolor on a classical theme, *Hebe Offering a Cup to the Eagle (Jove)*, was created by an English painter, William Hamilton, and made into a print by the English engraver Facius.[54] It became enormously popular in the Colonies and many of its derivatives have survived. In 1796 Edward Savage published an engraving of a now-lost painting called *Liberty in the Form of the Goddess of Youth Giving Support to the Bald Eagle*.[55] The engraving showed a monument supporting a flagstaff, with the Liberty Cap and flag of the United States pictured against a view of Boston's harbor, representing the welcomed evacuation of the British fleet. The Goddess of Liberty stands, supposedly, on Beacon Hill, where she tramples the key to the Bastille—a present from General Lafayette to General Washington—symbolizing the death of monarchial tyranny in France, and the Star of the Order of the Garter of Britain next to a broken chain symbolizing freedom from slavery. This engraving contained so many of the now totally accepted and loved symbols of the new land that it was copied all over the land in various media and interpretations (fig. 4). Thus Hebe had been transformed into an American called Liberty.

The newly freed country's ideals of liberty, independence, federal union, opportunity, and plenty were celebrated in an outpouring of national pride—the promise of American life under its new republican government was to be a beacon for all mankind. In the growing fervor to portray the young nation as a living entity, new crosscurrents of taste developed, and from 1783 to 1815, no single personification or symbol of America dominated. The Stars and Stripes became a popular motif, often accompanied by Washington or a representation of Liberty, backed by the Sons of Liberty or by an army; often Liberty held the new flag, a flag of her very own, expressing the maturing image of the young United States of America. This new Miss Liberty was often a manifestation of the Indian Princess; the Plumed Greek Goddess; the Goddess of Wisdom; Minerva; the Goddess of Liberty; or later, Columbia—forms sometimes used interchangeably. After the War of 1812, Brother or Cousin Jonathan and Uncle Sam enjoyed favor as symbols, but the female image remained strong.

Personifications of America were rarely used alone, and additional American symbols were added to enrich the potpourri of the already popular Liberty Cap, pole, eagle, and flag: the national motto, *E. Pluribus Unum*; the linked chain of states; the stars of the states; the Shield of thirteen stripes and stars; the date of independence, July 4, 1776; the Constitution, represented by a temple with thirteen columns for the thirteen states; altars and urns; George Washington, Thomas Jefferson, and Benjamin Franklin, evoking memories of heroes, statesmen and generals; Niagara Falls, sacred to some

Indian tribes in the East; the beehive, symbol of industry; palm and coconut trees reminiscent of the Indian Queen; cargo vessels of tobacco and cotton; expanses of wilderness; the globe; the rattlesnake; and the composite Indian/black boy.[56]

This curious young figure, sometimes garbed in Eastern drapery and turban or in American Indian feathers, reinstated the Indian elements that had disappeared from the dress of the Plumed Goddess. Although Indians had been taken to England, the English confused them with the blacks they knew from the Caribbean, as well as the African slaves imported to the New World. Like the cigar-store Indians of the United States, those carved black figures, dressed in feathers, marked tobacco shops in Europe—Europeans had embraced smoking for pleasure as well as for medicinal purposes. As these themes interchanged and crossed the Atlantic, the youth appeared in a toile made by Oberkampf between 1783 and 1790, *America Paying Homage to France*, counterpointing design elements among the new nation, Britain, and France.[57] He surfaced in other prints, paintings, needlework compositions, and sculptures, among them the watercolor *Memorial to General Washington*, c. 1815, in which he accompanies the Plumed Goddess (fig. 19).

Among the female figures, Columbia originally came to popular attention as a name proposed for the new nation, the feminine form of Christopher Columbus.[58] It first appeared in America in the *Phaenomena Quaedam Apocalyptica* of 1697, as the suggestion of Chief Justice Samuel Sewall of the Massachusetts Bay Colony, and then in England in the 1730s.[59] Washington's troops sang a song called "Columbia" and two American warships were so designated. In 1784 King's College in New York changed its name to Columbia, and the site of the new capital was the District of Columbia. Recalling the country's discovery and symbolizing the notion that America, through Columbus's voyage, linked the Occident to the Orient, the name spread to papers, magazines, towns, rivers, etc.

Columbia never wore feathers or ostrich plumes in her hair, and neither did she carry a bow and arrows.[60] The Liberty Cap and pole accompanied her as did the flag, the Shield, the Bald Eagle, the linked chain of states, the thirteen stars, and the dates of the Declaration of Independence and the formulation of the Constitution. Dressed in white, she wore the starred national banner across her chest. Originally bareheaded, she later wore a laurel wreath, a helmet, a tiara or occasionally a Liberty Cap over her sometimes classical coiffure. She

3. Artist unknown: *Africa–America*. London. 1808. Hand-colored mezzotint, 9¼″ x 13⅝″. *Africa–America*, from the set of *Four Continents* published by T. Hinton in London, shows the Indian Princess at the right wearing a large feathered headdress, flanked by two tomahawks, and guarded by a rattlesnake. She rides in a chariot drawn by tigers with Niagara Falls in the background and holds a fifteen-starred flag centered with a portrait of George Washington. Facing America is Africa at the left, symbolized by a black female in feathered headdress, seated in a chariot pulled by lions, and with native huts in the background. Africa holds a banner inscribed: *Slave Trade abolished in England 1806.* (Print Collection, The New York Public Library: Astor, Lenox and Tilden Foundations)

often merged with Minerva and Liberty by carrying a shield and spear, but her demeanor expressed more maturity, strength, dignity, serenity, and assurance. As early as 1786, she graced the frontispiece of *Columbia* magazine, along with Minerva; altars; globes; sailing ships; men plowing, symbolizing "Hands to work and hearts to God"; the rays of the rising sun; and a constellation of stars, as well as the familiar cornucopias, American Eagle, Liberty Caps and pole, and palm trees.[61]

Classical deities such as Minerva and the goddesses Justice, Truth, and Wisdom had limited uses, but not so Liberty—for it was the Goddess of Liberty who really progressed to become identified with the American cause. Despite her European past, commonly associated with the Liberty Cap and pole, she became completely identified with America. Liberty was constantly portrayed holding or dressed in the flag or supporting the American Shield, guarded by the American Eagle, or associated with the thirteen stars and stripes as well as the date July 4, 1776.[62]

It was Liberty who appeared on the first coins to be minted by the United States government, the cent and the half cent in 1793, and on the more valuable gold coins.[63] She became part of the architecture of the Capitol in 1817—a large plaster sculpture standing in flowing classical clothing, her extended right arm holding the Constitution,[64] with an American eagle guarding her right side while the rattlesnake or Serpent of Wisdom encircles a columnlike altar.

Among the four major personifications of the United States in the visual arts—the Indian Princess, the Plumed Greek Goddess, the American Goddess of Liberty, and Columbia—she would endure. The Plumed Goddess, the neoclassical fancy, had limited usefulness for interpreting America. The Indian Princess remained popular through the nineteenth century but became less identified with the spirit of the newly liberated land as Columbia, specifically created to represent the young nation, grew in popularity and use. But because Columbia—associated with peace, justice, plenty, wisdom, the arts and sciences, and liberty—did not convey any one dominant moral quality, a conviction began to surface that the young country, founded in a passionate ideal, should have a symbol for it. It was inevitable that, with increasing use, the American Liberty would become interchangeable with Columbia, an affinity occurring from 1815 to 1860.[65] It was also inevitable that in the competition for public favor Liberty would win.

The new machine age of the mid-1800s was the era of the common man, with an increase in leisure time and an emergence of the individual that brought American folk art into flower. This "By the People, for the People" energetic art encompassed an infinite variety of media: engravings, maps, weathervanes, tavern signs, ship figureheads, cigar-store figures, scrimshaw, watercolor and oil paintings, various forms of needlework, woven and printed textiles, quilts, hooked rugs, banners, metalwork, sculptures of all kinds, cake molds and cookie cutters, handmade dolls and toys—one kind of art influencing the other.

America's heartfelt identification with Liberty and her female image increasingly became an inspiration for artists, craftspeople, and folk artists. Plain and fancy American folk art pieces, generally one-of-a-kind, made by hand, revealed personal visions of their untutored creators—imaginative, eccentric, spontaneous, and original artworks created for utilitarian, decorative, religious, economic, personal, or political use. This intuitive art, made from found and recycled materials, with its faulty perspective, bright colors, and pattern and detail emphasis often threw conventional rules of composition and realism to the winds. It was an emotionally powerful art, with roots more often in the country than in the city; close to the craft tradition but sometimes emulating fine art.

Even popular art, mass produced by hand or machine and intended for mass viewing or consumption, echoed the new patriotic iconography. Various depictions of the "fine female figure" appeared on glassware, such as a flask with the profile of Liberty wearing her cap (fig. 79); cast iron, coins of the realm, carousel and circus carvings, stamps, and furniture made by such leading cabinetmakers as Samuel McIntire, including mirror frames and clock cases. Americans of all degrees of sophistication, education, and wealth loved their new country with unabashed abandon and wanted its symbols, capturing the fresh and high ideals of liberty, freedom, and equality for all, to be part of their everyday life, both inside and outside.

American folk painting recorded the New World in portraits; in land- and seascapes; in scenes inspired by religion, history, remembrances of the Old World; and after freedom was won and independence established, American heroes and political symbols. Utilitarian objects—signs, fireboards, mantels, room ends, floors and floor coverings, window shades, walls, ceilings, furniture, and other everyday implements—were decorated by self-taught peripatetic painters called limners, who supported themselves in their travels by bartering their art for bed and board. Other folk painters were isolated, localized artists who simply created their personal visions for their own pleasure and need.

Some of these seemingly spontaneous ink drawings, watercolors, and oil paintings had their origins in early prints, in fine art, in art manuals, and later, in photography. With the growth and prosperity of the young nation, some artists had instruction in drawing and painting. As education became more widely available, young girls in seminaries began to study art—copying prints, for the most part—creating such watercolor and oil paintings as mourning scenes and theorem pictures, making reverse paintings on glass, and using tinsel and marble dust/sandpaper techniques with painstaking pinpricking to add textural and pattern interest. Watercolor and oil paintings were sometimes combined with needlework, resulting in unique, original, and personal interpretations.

During the Federal period, countless prints, from both England and America, celebrated the young country's growing strength and nationalism—among them the engraving by Edward Savage. Based on Hamilton's painting *Hebe Offering a Cup to the Eagle (Jove)*, it proved to be a seminal influence on American patriotic art. *Liberty in the Form of the Goddess of Youth Giving Support to the Bald Eagle*, by Abijah Canfield (1769–1830), done in Chusetown, Connecticut, c. 1800, was inspired by the engraving, as clearly stated by the artist.[66] It is one of the very few known American examples of this subject done as a reverse painting on glass, a technique learned from the Orient via the busy trade of the times (fig. 5).

In Savage's engraving, a barefooted, blue-sashed, flower-garlanded, white-gowned Liberty tramples symbols of tyranny—the key, the broken chain, and the star—as she gives the American Bald Eagle nourishment from a cup in her right hand. The American Flag, Liberty Cap, and pole are visible in the background emerging from clouds, while Boston harbor is viewed in the distance. Rays of sunlight emanate from behind the eagle. Dark-haired Liberty has beautiful, clearly defined features and is dressed in a lacy Grecian toga over a draped skirt. Although Savage clearly described the work in his exhibition catalogue, even the academic artists of the day felt free to use their imagination, particularly in the lower left area, where a lake, flowers, doves, ships, houses, walking people, trees, and arches could be added. However, the same theme, Liberty nourishing the American Eagle, remained constant.

One delightful work that Savage's engraving inspired,

Liberty and Washington, appeared on a window shade, one of eleven painted for a Connecticut tavern; it is a somewhat refreshing, innocent version incorporating the Liberty Tree, the Liberty Cap and pole, and a bust of George Washington, but the eagle flies overhead as Liberty's right hand is not free to offer a cup[67] (fig. 8). Quite different is an oil on canvas of *Liberty*, with its eagle having changed direction and Liberty's attire being somewhat daring, for she wears a slit skirt revealing high-laced sandals (fig. 9). A paint-on-velvet copy may have been created with stencils. The artist probably misunderstood the directions, for the lines of Liberty's footwear are painted blue (fig. 10). In another interpretation, *Emblem of the United States of America*, a crowned Liberty sits on the globe beside a plow and shield, pointing to clipper ships coming home (fig. 11). Still another oil entitled *Centennial Progress USA July 4, 1876*, includes faces of all the presidents to 1886 in a boat carved with wooden eagles (fig. 12). Liberty, draped in a flag, gazes toward the wilderness, protected by the hovering eagle and accompanied by an Indian brave. *Pater Patriae*, a reverse painting on glass, was taken from an engraving that was made from a painting, continuing the borrowing from different media and the juxtaposition of the changing images of America (fig. 6). A large tomahawk emphasizes a powerful, protective image of Liberty in an oil signed *L.N.* (fig. 13).

America's penchant for taking "liberties with Liberty" is shown in watercolors ranging from a bareheaded, simply draped *Columbia at Niagara Falls*, holding a scrolled paper (fig. 20); to *America*, a more fashionable Liberty in a sashed and ruffled dress and an upswept hairstyle, glaring at a cowering lion and female figure of Britain while the Bald Eagle emits lightning bolts (fig. 16). A gentle, dark-haired *Emblem of Peace* stands amid stylized morning-glories (fig. 18), while an unusual blond *Columbia* wears a laurel wreath in her hair and coral beads around her neck to ward off evil, a superstition from Europe (fig. 21). A rattlesnake and sequins are oddly compatible features of a watercolor attributed to Betsey B. Lathrop (fig. 15). *Our Country Is Free* is a delicate version of a Currier and Ives print (fig. 23). Another *Miss Liberty* in a bonnet with streamers wears fetching hosiery with tiny pinpricked clocks and holds a palm leaf (fig. 17). A drawing by the Virginia artist Lewis Miller shows a smiling Columbia embracing a helmeted figure (fig. 7).

The impact of Savage's engraving on nonacademic artists created a legacy of highly varied folk art in a wide spectrum of media, including needlework. Sewing was a vital skill for both sexes, as the basic need to clothe, to protect, and to maintain their environment was paramount in the harsh days of the early settlements. With the growth and prosperity of the young democracy, needleworkers could turn their attention to samplers, progressing to more complicated pieces. Love of country and the need to create beautiful, useful items culminated in many diverse stitcheries, some being versions of Savage's engraving.

One of the earliest needleworks shows the Indian Princess with two pilgrims, animals, and very large strawberries (fig. 30). A later embroidery on muslin, crude and stained with age, shows the Indian Princess holding the American flag and leaning on an anchor, the symbol of hope (fig. 32). Savage's influence is also seen in the imaginative silk, watercolor, mica, and sequins on silk embroidery showing *Liberty in Front of the Trenton Arches* (fig. 33). His theme of Liberty giving sustenance to the eagle appears in *Memorial to Washington*, which has a stitched and painted, dark-ringleted Liberty with personalized additions of a house, people walking, and trees (fig. 34). Folk memory retained certain elements of Savage's work long after it had ceased to have a direct influence. As new elements entered, eventually American versions, with their changes of detail, mood, and media, became hybrids, almost unrecognizable. One extraordinary needlework, *Liberty and Washington Memorial*, of silk, chenille, and paint on silk shows a blond Indian girl seated under a spreading Liberty Tree gazing at Benjamin Franklin and a haloed George Washington while the sun sets, symbolizing Washington's death (fig. 31).

The lineage of weathervanes is ancient, with the earliest recorded example being of a triton—half man, half fish—in Greece. In America, however, the design of weathervanes reached unique and beautiful heights. Weathervanes were essential in gauging wind direction and velocity, vital for seafaring and agricultural needs—for survival—but they were also symbolic of the social and political equality found in the New World. In America anyone who could make or buy a vane could have an emblem over his home or farm that evoked the status formerly shown by the banners of the nobility, the clergy, and other prominent people of Europe. At first individually made and later factory produced to meet the growing demand, vanes varied in design according to the time and talents their makers could devote to them or according to the materials at hand, such as wood, copper, brass, zinc, and lead, and paint and gilding.

One of the first designs used was the American Indian brave, and his feathered arrow carried over into many of the Columbia and Liberty vanes. A. K. Jewell and Company of Waltham, Massachusetts, was the first factory to show a vane of Columbia and her flag in its one-sheet catalogue of 1860.[68] Some vanes were gilded or polychromed, with cutout stars and stripes, and were impressed with the maker's name and patent. Time and erosion by the elements blurred many original crisp vane designs but, in compensation, weathered their original bright surfaces into interesting, textured patinas. They often suffered punctures as well—probably from young boys trying out their first guns, for most weathervanes flashing in the wind must have proved irresistible targets.

One of the earliest Liberty vanes features a small but charming goddess with punched stars in the flag (fig. 35). A larger version with red, white, and blue emblazoned on the flag, appears faceless (fig. 36). Another contains fasces, the bundle of rods—another classical motif merging into our political iconography—that were originally carried before magistrates in ancient Rome as a symbol of authority.[69] A gilded Liberty in Liberty Cap stands by her fasces (fig. 37). Vanes changed as costumes and hairstyles evolved, as shown by a Liberty figure with long tresses flying in the wind and an unusual skirt (fig. 38). A wooden weathervane pattern, painted white and gold, with a wreath encircling a classical hairstyle, served as a model for a Columbia vane[70] (fig. 39). In the chauvinistic nineteenth century, other symbols of freedom proliferated—the rattlesnake, the Liberty Cap, the eagle, Columbia, or the Goddess of Liberty.

Carving, too, began almost immediately in the Colonies, as settlers had to make virtually everything then needed, both useful and decorative objects, by hand. Some artists' names were recorded, but most decorative carvings existing today were created by anonymous sailors, blacksmiths, tinsmiths, farmers, itinerant artists and carpenters, lumberjacks, boatbuilders, ornamental carvers—anyone who wanted to whittle away the time. Wood carvings were made to attract migrating birds for food; to embellish inns, taverns, and ships; for circus and carousel decoration; to make pastry imprints; to mark burial places; to decorate buildings and homes; to create toys; even to record private visions and political imagery. The young country had enormous virgin forests with a wide variety of woods, and its forms—knots and twisted branches, even its grain—sometimes dictated design and function.

4. Edward Savage: *Liberty in the Form of the Goddess of Youth Giving Support to the Bald Eagle*. United States. 1796. Steel engraving, 25″ x 16½″. Based on an earlier academic painting of the Greek goddess Hebe and the god Jove, who was traditionally symbolized by the eagle, this engraving inspired a great number of folk-art renditions unifying Liberty, the eagle, the flag, the Liberty cap and pole, and the Old World symbols of tyranny—the key to the Bastille, the crown of Britain, the broken chain, and the star of the Order of the Garter. The engraving was widely circulated and admired and copied in watercolor, paintings on velvet, and reverse paintings on glass, both here and in the Orient for the American market. (New York State Historical Association, Cooperstown, New York)

5. Abijah Canfield: *Liberty in the Form of the Goddess of Youth Giving Support to the Bald Eagle*. Chusetown, Connecticut. c. 1800. Reverse painting (gouache) on glass, 24³⁄₁₆″ x 18⁷⁄₁₆″. Countless prints celebrating the growing strength of the United States circulated both in this country and abroad during the early Federal period. Some of these reached China via merchant ships and were freely copied by Oriental artists using the technique of reverse painting on glass. This is one of the very few American examples known, and the artist clearly states at the bottom that his source of design was the engraving by E. Savage. (Greenfield Village and Henry Ford Museum, Dearborn, Michigan)

Inspired American woodcarvers copied depictions of heroes and patriotic symbols—from prints or even from academic art; from broadsides, documents, coins, and three-dimensional representations; from inn, shop, and tavern signs; from weathervanes; and a myriad of sources—carving their very own Miss Liberties, Columbias, American Eagles, George Washingtons, and finally, the Statue of Liberty herself. Our true first lady of the land was carved in an enormous variety of styles, woods, and poses throughout two centuries, all reinforcing the idea of freedom.

Among their creations were figureheads. How the custom of using figureheads on ships evolved may never be known, but it is an ancient practice. Egyptians had carved birds and banners on boats as early as 4000 B.C. The Vikings traveled far in their sailing vessels carved with geometrics and mystical animals. From the early "evil eye" to geometric carvings progressing to more defined designs, carvings on ships' prows were amulets or talismans to get the ship safely to port. So powerful were these symbols that the ship would head homeward if anything went awry with its figurehead. Later figureheads were used to identify as were flags of their countries of origin. Following the American Revolution, a wide variety of political symbols identified the ships of the new nation—the eagle, early patriots, Columbia, and Liberty, who symbolized not only a free nation but that the United States' sailing fleet believed in free trade and sailor's rights.[71] One beautiful surviving figurehead, weathered and cracked from trade winds and salty seas, features Liberty with torch in hand (fig. 42).

On smaller waterways, too, carved wooden figures and their metal siblings were used as figureheads on steamboats, ferries, and pilot boats. Interpretations were diverse—the serenity of a blue-garbed, blond-tressed Columbia deck figure holding the orb of the world (fig. 46) seems a far cry from the smaller but fierce Miss Liberty from a boathouse in New Hampshire[72] (fig. 47).

Carvers also fashioned shop markers and signs. It is not known when the first trade symbol and shop sign appeared in the Colonies, but the custom was well established in Europe as well as in the Orient. Towns in France, Austria, and Switzerland still have their original although timeworn signs hanging before old shops on narrow streets as yet untouched by "progress"—more graceful and inviting than any gaudy, blinking neon could ever be. In America after the early East Coast settlements grew into towns and cities, all sorts of businesses and tradesmen appeared, fulfilling the growing needs of a burgeoning economy. Main Street, often the only street in town, was patterned with a crazy quilt of highly colored, variously shaped signs.

Weathervanes capping church spires were the highest and most visible "signs." For more temporal needs, the barber, the tanner, the apothecary, the shoemaker, the hatter, the tailor, the cabinetmaker, the joiner, the grain dealer, the chemist, the blacksmith, the livery, the textile manufacturer, the nautical supplier, and the fishmonger (if near the sea), and the tavern (for needs of a different spirit) all had easily understood symbols relating what they sold. Patriotic carvings were rarely used as cigar-store front or countertop figures, but there are surviving examples of the Indian Princess advertising tobacco—one of the female image of America's first affiliations (fig. 43).

The first signs were three-dimensional, created by local or itinerant carvers, painters, or blacksmiths. These three-dimensional signs evolved into flat signboards, either semifree swinging models or signs on stationary stands, with a symbol and a name on both sides to attract customers coming or going.[73] Landscapes, portraits, decorative motifs, animals, and political ideas were related to different types of merchandise, retail services, houses, toll signs, inns, and taverns.[74]

Many pre-Revolutionary loyalists displayed the likenesses of English royalty, the lion of Britain, and loyalist politicians. As the political climate heated with the rise of rebellion, the idea of liberty flourished and symbols of freedom appeared throughout the country. One oil-on-canvas over pine sign, baroque in outline, dating from 1860 in Connecticut, shows Liberty nourishing the eagle—yet another echo of Savage's influence[75] (fig. 44). Savage's work was known even as far afield as Ohio and can be seen in a three-dimensional sign found over an office of a justice of the peace[76] (fig. 45). Another very unusual sign depicting Liberty in her Liberty Cap has survived from Bissell's Tavern in Connecticut and is dated 1801.[77]

Other carvings wound up as architectural decorations or even parade figures. One surviving *Columbia* holding a scabbard may have been copied from a metal Demuth sculpture (fig. 48). The head of a small, nineteenth-century *Liberty*, remarkably like that of the Cabbage Patch dolls, has holes in its base and was probably a small parade figure displayed and carried during the Centennial era and later during Fourth of July celebrations. A small amazonian, classically coifed Columbia holds a flag (fig. 55), while the unpainted *Liberty with Flag* is handsomely enveloped by the flag (fig. 49).

Another wooden *Columbia* is carved and painted to resemble cast iron, possibly influenced by the popular metal sculptures seen on lawns, boats, building finials, and recess decorations[78] (fig. 56). A seated, diademed Liberty with a dog, created by an Italian immigrant, was probably inspired by religious processional or cathedral art[79] (fig. 54).

With the rapid growth of the iron industry, ferromania became the rage, yielding an incredible array of articles such as a rare *Birth of a Nation* stove figure used as a radiator (fig. 51). A crowned metal head is all that survives of a lost statue from Pennsylvania (fig. 52). Indoors, a pair of andirons brought Liberty to the fireplace (fig. 53).

The story of the circus in America shimmers with images of ornamented wagons, elephants, bearded ladies, clowns, wild animals in cages, hit-the-target games, "fishy" mermaids, hootchy-kootchy girls swaying in veils, twirling carousels, and trapeze artists. The oom-pah-pah of the steam calliope; the prancing, performing horses; excited spectators, children, and barking dogs hailed the parade from the railroad yard to the big tent. Wood carving served a special function in this tinsel-and-glitter world. Circus wagons, part of that passing parade, were extravagantly adorned and garishly colored to catch the eye. But beneath all that razzamatazz were beautifully carved allegorical figures from legends, animals, historical heroes, orientalia, and patriotic symbols. Often a "United States" wagon featured a Greek Goddess of Liberty flanked by two Indian maidens in feathered skirt and headdress, holding tomahawks and feathered Liberty Poles and Liberty Caps.[80] A Columbia from an inside chariot panel of the Olympic Park Carousel in New Jersey sits amid a rising sun, the swirling flag, and the eagle.[81] A broadside, *Miss America on a Tightrope*, was printed from a wood block and probably colored patriotically to catch attention, heralding the arrival of a circus (fig. 66).

Political symbols also became important in textile design, both here and abroad. Americans enjoyed hanging, wearing, and sitting on fabrics that reminded them of their nation. The invention of copper-plate printing in England and France in the second half of the eighteenth century made large-scale furnishing fabrics available, with monochromatic hues printed on neutral backgrounds of linen and cotton. The images of America are encompassed in the beautiful toile called *Apotheosis of George Washington and Benjamin Franklin*, in which almost all the symbols occur[82] (fig. 67). A textile printed later shows the Statue of Liberty set in scattered stars, with medallions of George Washington alternating with Columbus discovering America, a map of the Americas, and the United States Capitol.

The idea of freedom was not restricted to printed textiles. Coverlets made by both professional weavers and housewives incorporated designs derived from weaving drafts exchanged throughout the States, with each weaver leaving his or her individualistic mark. A double-weave red and white Jacquard coverlet of cotton and wool, dated 1849, has four Liberty heads surrounding a floral center medallion[83] (fig. 69). Another coverlet has four Indian Princess figures and eagles holding banners inscribed *Hail Columbia* (fig. 68).

Even the culinary arts would incorporate Liberty motifs. Cookie and cake boards, used to shape and beautify breads and pastries, developed from a variety of cultural traditions traceable through pagan and Christian Rome to the cults of ancient Greece and to the philosophies of the Persian Gulf.[84] Eucharistic bread stamps were used in Cyprus as early as the sixth century; molds of fired clay were popular throughout the Middle Ages.[85] There were wooden molds, too, known as springerle or marzipan, that emerged during the 1500s. The custom of using molds and stamps spread throughout the United States with the influx of English and European settlers.[86]

Admiration of Liberty permeated the culinary artifacts of young America, and many examples of "kitchen art" remain today. One cake board shows an Indian Princess holding a parrot, an heirloom from the Yates family (fig. 70). The *Washington Memorial Cake Board* shows Liberty giving a hovering eagle a cup of nourishment, illustrating again the great influence of the Savage engraving[87] (fig. 71). A rare tin cookie cutter bears the profile of Liberty with a classical hair arrangement (fig. 72).

Other special kinds of equipment were also adorned with Liberty's image. From the water-bucket brigade to twentieth-century technology, the history of fire-fighting has yielded an amazing legacy of paraphernalia, including firemen's hats, silver and brass horns, bells, pump wagons, water kegs, shields, hose holders, fire hydrants, horse trappings, weathervanes, paintings, firemarks, and engravings. Old hand- and horse-drawn, hand-pumped fire engines, used by the early volunteer fire departments of the 1800s, were named for famous contemporary or historical personages and sumptuously decorated with such patriotic symbols as Liberty[88]— especially the Greek Goddess of Liberty with her eagle, shield, Liberty Cap, and pole.[89] One decorated felt firehat worn on special occasions features Columbia perched on a rocky shore (fig. 73), and a handsome panel depicts Hebe feeding Zeus (fig. 74). A cast-iron Liberty profile with flowers in her hair is thought to be a firemark, to be placed on front exterior walls for quick identification.

Often Liberty appeared in a purely decorative context as well. *Scherenschnitte*—paper cutting—was a favorite pastime of eighteenth- and nineteenth-century ladies, whose education was not considered complete without instruction in needlework, drawing, painting, and related "minor arts."[90] These decorative paper cutout scenes of biblical, animal, sentimental, and patriotic themes were created with a painstaking, precise technique. The design was usually drawn on a folded sheet of paper, cut with sharp scissors or a blade and then unfolded to show delicate openwork, sometimes further embellished with color and pinpricks.[91] A mirror-backed *Washington Memorial*, illustrating this lacy technique, shows Liberty under a willow tree, symbol of death[92] (fig. 75).

Other decorative techniques also incorporated the Liberty emblem. Lonely, idle hours aboard ship gave sailors, away from home and loved ones for very long periods, the opportunity to carve bits of whalebone and teeth—an art form called scrimshaw—as gifts for family and friends. Familiar designs and patriotic motifs were comforting reminders of safety and home, offering a sort of sanity at sea. The delightful diversity of objects they produced include ditty boxes, swifts, busks, bodkins, jagging wheels, walking sticks, dice, dolls, dominoes, inkstands, toys, pipe tampers, seals, spool holders, rope guides, pickwicks, rolling laundry forks, bird cages, and knitting needles. One unusual helmeted Columbia scrimshaw is carved in bold relief, instead of the usual incised and inked technique (fig. 77). A rare tooth, dated 1847, shows Liberty and the eagle with mermaid tails, a Liberty Cap, and a tiger clawing a tree (fig. 76).

Although now an ever-present emblem in folk art, Miss Liberty gained a new importance during the nineteenth century as a staple of advertising art. Recognizing the public's fondness for national symbols, entrepreneurs were quick to use these motifs to sell products and services. The early affinity of tobacco and the Indian Princess continued with Miss Liberty in the early years of industrial growth and the development of color lithography. Cigar-box labels began to feature traditional Liberty figures, dressed in Liberty Cap and sandals, carrying the shield and laurel wreath, but sometimes joined by her now-distant relative, the feathered Indian Princess, who recalled the old cigar-store figure. On one cigar label, Liberty is flanked by two Indian children, each holding a tobacco leaf, while cargo ships are seen in the background harbor (fig. 84).

In the late nineteenth century, when the people of France endowed America with a concrete embodiment of Liberty—a permanent personification of a hundred years of images and inspirations—the impact was felt immediately. As Marvin Trachtenberg has noted in his book, *The Statue of Liberty*, she was higher than the Colossus of Rhodes and the other ancient wonders that constituted her monumental lineage. Thirty people could stand inside her head, while her torch could accommodate twelve;[93] her fingernail was twelve inches high and ten inches wide. She was greater than the Queen of the fourth continent, the Western Hemisphere; now the seven rays of her crown showed her dominion over the seven continents and the seven seas of the earth.[94] The tablet in her left hand implied the Mosaic tradition, promising justice and equality under the law, and bore the date of the Declaration of Independence in Roman numerals. Her torch stood for truth, freedom of the press, and free speech—the light of knowledge. She became a magnificent icon, a powerful new symbol to inspire the art of the nation's second century.

That is not to say that her image was entirely noble. The Statue of Liberty appeared in advertisements for kitchen ranges, sewing thread, paint, pens, circuses, theaters, toys, and innumerable other items. Somehow she still retained her connection to the tobacco industry—as recently as 1975, appearing in an ad, published by Liggett and Myers, that associated smoking with our concept of personal liberty.

Twentieth-century painters have re-created the Statue of Liberty's image in buttons, acrylics, enamels, plastic, metal, paper, and collages. *Liberty in the Palm of My Hand* features a blond mermaid holding a tiny Statue of Liberty (fig. 26). A collage has a French airplane, a boat from Britain, three tiny ducks, and a three-dimensional American flag (fig. 27), and a serene blue *Mother of Exiles* waves to boatloads of tourists (fig. 28). Contemporary sculptures of the Statue of Liberty incorporated, as did sculptures in the past, found and recycled materials, bright colors, and the individualistic spark that engenders unique works. One Liberty made from a pole has her very own cannon and a heart-shaped shield[95] (fig. 58). *Miss Liberty*, inspired by a picture of a cast-metal Statue of Liberty, is comfortably attired in a togalike flag and T-shirt, and brightly painted toenails make her especially fetching[96] (fig. 64). On a more

TRENTON
PRINCETOWN
MONMOUTH
YORKTOWN.

PATER
PATRIÆ.

Sacred to the Memory of the
truly Illustrious
GEORGE WASHINGTON. Renowned in
War Great in the Senate, and
pofsefsed of every Qualification
to render him worthy the Title of
a GREAT and GOOD MAN.

BORN Feb 22 1732. Ob. Dec. 14. 1799.

6. Attributed to Vecchio: *Pater Patriae*. New York. c. 1800. Reverse painting on glass, 14⅛″ x 10⅜″. Fame blows her trumpet while Minerva in a plumed helmet holds George Washington's portrait in this splendid memorial to our first president. Columbia has a spear and a shield and a weeping soldier mourns, as cupids bear emblems of war and liberty. The memorial originally belonged to the Barton family of Boston and was based on Enoch G. Gridley's engraving, issued in 1800, derived from a painting by John Coles, Jr. (The Metropolitan Museum of Art, New York; gift of Edgar William and Bernice Chrysler Garbisch, 1964)

poignant note, a tall, gilded, wooden Statue of Liberty was carved in gratitude by an East German refugee, reaffirming the synthesis of liberty and America (fig. 62). A strongly crafted and striking Liberty stands on a Denver street to remind students to help fund the Statue's refurbishing (fig. 65).

Twentieth-century folk artists, too, have created their own interpretations, as did folk artists of the past. One of the most fascinating examples is a whirligig weather-vane showing men busily restoring her for the upcoming Centennial celebration (fig. 41). And a touching twentieth-century crocheted version of the Statue of Liberty created by a German immigrant shows the need to assert love of country using whatever techniques, materials, and talent are available. A recent paper cutting of many Statues of Liberty surrounded by many American flags and Americans of all sizes and shapes continues this tradition.

Scrap wood shavings have been recycled into golden curls for a hefty, blue-eyed Statue of Liberty (fig. 60). Metal remnants, paint, and dangling earrings were transformed into a heavily mascaraed *New York Lady* sculpture, which has only six rays in her crown (fig. 63). A small bronze dinner bell summoned a Rhode Island family to dinner, where they could have partaken of their very own Statue of Liberty ice cream, formed in a pewter mold (fig. 83). For after-dinner entertainment, the group could have gazed through the family's old kaleidoscope, with a hand-painted image of Liberty (fig. 82). Fourth of July fireworks blossom in the skies over the Statue of Liberty in Kathy Jakobsen's sparkling painting (fig. 29). Private visions, beyond the immediate grasp of others, now called "outsider art" have been part of every culture. The *Lady Liberty of 1953*, jetting through blue skies, is a very personal image of freedom (fig. 24).

Of course, she has not lost her political significance. Colorful posters, so popular toward the end of the nineteenth century, became more so during World War I, when Miss Liberty joined America's entire family of political symbols calling Americans to "duty" for special causes. She urged the planting of gardens in the "Sow the Seeds of Victory" campaign. A strong image of Liberty also appeared with a Boy Scout in a poster for a World War I loan campaign drive and inspired an artist to copy it (fig. 87). An early money box of jigsawed wood was used to collect donations for construction of her base (fig. 59). But she still had her detractors: Howard Chandler Christy drew her as one of his

"Christy Girls," a Grecian-garbed glamour girl anticipating Miss America, replacing the more remote, modest, and dignified Statue of Liberty. A cartoon of the early 1970s shows Miss Liberty onstage with Uncle Sam, being pelted with rotten tomatoes for giving a "bad performance"[97] (fig. 88).

While some folk art of considerable charm is inspired by honest patriotism and the "loving hands of home," tasteless kitsch, manufactured in a totally unharnessed commercial spirit continues to proliferate. Metal savings banks and gaudy plastic red, white, and blue Statue of Liberty replicas; mugs with the Campbell's Soup Kids dressed as the Statue of Liberty; bath and dish towels, T-shirts, postcards, bar accessories, ashtrays, electric light, *Mad* magazines, thermometers, night-lights equating her torch with an ice-cream cone (fig. 90), even New York street signs—the list is endless—show how the indiscriminate use of political symbols and monuments as decoration without iconographic content robs them of dignity and power.

This mighty Mother of Exiles is the famed and beloved sign of America's high ideals, her many freedoms, and her quest for a true democracy, constantly vigilant against oppression and aggression. The desire still persists to use her image to express love of freedom and love of country, whether in homemade copies cherished in Small Town, U.S.A.; in drawings, paintings, children's games, a cloth doll (fig. 80), sheet-music covers, a stained glass window (fig. 86), or in tacky souvenirs.

And so she appears in the informative 1984 Chemical Bank calendar; as a twenty-six-inch bronze sculpture, created by Erte to be sold in limited editions to help fund her refurbishing and that of Ellis Island; as an enormous "chocolate" made by a confectioner from Spain (fig. 94); on the cover of a cheerful advertisement from Bloomingdale's department store, showing her as a pastry chef presiding over a birthday cake amid food processors and icing tubes; as a chubby, carved wood-and-iron gate finial found in Delaware (fig. 57); as the title of a Broadway musical; as a line of note cards; as a small replica near Lincoln Center and, of course, in smaller scale near the Eiffel Tower in Paris.

The Statue of Liberty was a movie star in *The Planet of the Apes*; in the final scene she was partially submerged on a desolate beach after a nuclear holocaust. License has even been taken by the New York State Motor Vehicle Bureau, which wants her image on all license plates in celebration of her Centennial, despite an editorial pleading for restraint and taste. And yet,

7. Lewis Miller: *Peace* from *Orbis Pictus*. United States. c. 1849. Drawing, 9⅜″ x 7⅞″. Columbia, holding the American shield, stresses peace as she embraces a helmeted female figure. Blindfolded Justice with scales and sword fronts a Liberty monument topped by an American eagle on an urn. (Abby Aldrich Rockefeller Folk Art Center, Williamsburg, Virginia)

8. Artist unknown: *Liberty and Washington*. United States. 1800–1810. Oil on windowshade, 74″ x 44″. All the current elements of American iconography are seen in this anonymous painting, one of eleven that hung in a Connecticut tavern. Although based on Savage's *Liberty*, this Liberty has a rosy-cheeked, youthful face. (New York State Historical Association)

who can resist a smile when cranky Lucy of the *Peanuts* comic strip, dressed as the Statue of Liberty, crown askew, pleads for children to help in funding of the Statue's restoration.

There are those who find it crass to put the Statue of Liberty on a license plate, to become dirty and dented. There are those who believe that Mom's apple pie is mostly store bought now, frozen in plastic; that our heritage is commercialized with slick restorations everywhere and reproduction folk art "made in Taiwan"; that in promoting twentieth-century folk art, we are creating the very conditions that will deface or even destroy it. But a funny thing is happening on the way to the end of the twentieth century. Patriotism once again is becoming acceptable.

In this age of terrorism and nuclear tension, of life under the sea and out in space, Americans have been made more aware of the many freedoms enjoyed here in these United States—the freedom to be anything you want, anytime, anywhere; the freedom to create anything you want, anytime, anywhere.

The Statue of Liberty is still the symbol of freedom, whether to homeless Vietnamese children, to Cambodian boat people, to "wetbacks," or to the family next door. Who knows what will be added to our heritage of political folk art as these new "Americans" from Haiti, Japan, Cuba, China, the Near East, and Central and South America take their "liberties with Liberty." The desire to express love of country still exists.

If it is true that man-made monuments are visual reminders of shared ideas—the memories and hopes of an entire society—and are chosen by that society as part of its collective image, continuing to inspire, then a monument can become a patriotic symbol, reflecting pride and deep love of country.

If a patriotic symbol can permeate a society's psyche to such great depth that instant recognition connotes its meaning—liberty—and it is re-created over and over by many people at different times, then this symbol has become part of the "stream of consciousness" of that society.

If it is true that folk art reflects that undercurrent, then it must be true that the Statue of Liberty has become monumental folk art.

But whether in long curls, coiffured, Liberty Capped or crowned; whether feathered, draped, or gowned; this supreme icon of America has always been a favorite subject for American folk artists—and naturally so, for the folk art of America has *always* reflected what is important to her people.

This "fine female figure," foremost Lady of the Land, is a constant reminder to all that America is still "at liberty."

NOTES

1. Robert Gambee, *Manhattan Seascape: Waterside Views Around New York* (New York: Hastings House, 1975), p. 32.
2. William Koehlling, "History of the Statue of Liberty, New York," *Oculus* (February 1984), p. 1.
3. Marvin Trachtenberg, *The Statue of Liberty* (New York: The Viking Press, 1976), pp. 70, 87.
4. Ibid., p. 71.
5. Ibid., p. 63.
6. Ibid.
7. Chemical Bank Calendar, 1984.
8. Ibid.
9. Ibid.
10. Koehlling, "History of the Statue of Liberty," p. 1.
11. E. McClung Fleming, "The American Image as Indian Princess, 1765–1783," *Winterthur Portfolio II* (1965), p. 66.
12. Ibid., p. 65.
13. Ibid.
14. Ibid.

15. Ibid.

16. Lynette I. Rhodes, *American Folk Art from the Traditional to the Naive* (Cleveland, Ohio: The Cleveland Museum of Art, 1978), p. 89.

17. Fleming, "American Image," p. 67.

18. Ibid.

19. Ibid., pp. 67, 68.

20. Ibid.

21. Ibid.

22. Ibid., p. 69.

23. Ibid.

24. Ibid., p. 70.

25. Ibid.

26. Ibid., p. 71.

27. Ibid., pp. 74, 76.

28. Ibid., p. 77.

29. Ibid., p. 73.

30. Ibid., p. 71.

31. Ibid., p. 74.

32. Louis C. Jones, *Outward Signs of Inner Beliefs: Symbols of American Patriotism* (Cooperstown, N.Y.: New York State Historical Association, 1975), p. 3.

33. Fleming, "American Image," p. 74.

34. Ibid.

35. Ibid.

36. Elinor Lander Horwitz, *The Bird, the Banner and Uncle Sam* (Philadelphia and New York: J.B. Lippincott, 1976), p. 27.

37. Jones, *Outward Signs,* p. 71.

38. Susan H. Anderson, *The Most Splendid Carpet* (Philadelphia: National Park Service, U.S. Department of the Interior, 1978), p. 54.

39. Ibid.

40. Jones, *Outward Signs,* p. 27.

41. Ibid., p. 5.

42. Ibid.

43. Fleming, "American Image," p. 77.

44. Jones, *Outward Signs,* p. 4.

45. Ibid., p. 5.

46. Anderson, *Most Splendid Carpet,* p. 54.

47. E. McClung Fleming, "From Indian Princess to Greek Goddess, The American Image, 1783–1815," *Winterthur Portfolio III* (1967), p. 50.

48. Ibid., p. 46.

49. Henry Dreyfuss, *Symbol Sourcebook* (New York: McGraw-Hill, 1972), p. 18.

50. Ibid., p. 119.

51. Ibid.

52. Fleming, "Indian Princess," p. 51.

53. Jones, *Outward Signs,* p. 5.

54. Ibid.

55. Ibid.

56. Fleming, "Indian Princess," pp. 38, 39.

57. Ibid., p. 45.

58. Ibid., p. 59.

59. Ibid.

60. Ibid.

61. Ibid., p. 60.

62. Ibid., p. 56.

63. Ibid.

64. Ibid., p. 58.

65. Ibid., p. 66.

66. Robert Bishop, *Folk Painters of America* (New York: E.P. Dutton, 1979), plate 8.

67. Jones, *Outward Signs,* p. 7.

68. Ruth Andrews, *How to Know American Folk Art* (New York: E.P. Dutton, 1977), p. 170.

69. Robert Bishop and Patricia Coblentz, *A Gallery of American Weathervanes and Whirligigs* (New York: E.P. Dutton, 1981), p. 49.

70. Shelburne Museum, (FW-104) Sheet.

71. Marian and Charles Klamkin, *Wood Carvings, North American Folk Sculptures* (New York: Hawthorn Books, 1974), p. 7.

72. Bishop and Coblentz, *Weathervanes and Whirligigs,* p. 230.

73. Clarence P. Hornung, *Treasury of American Design and Antiques* (New York: Harry N. Abrams, 1950), p. 72.

74. Ibid., p. 73.

75. Louis C. Jones, "Liberty and Considerable License," *Antiques* (July 1958), p. 43.

76. Jones, *Outward Signs,* front and back cover and p. 70.

77. Hornung, *Treasury of American Design,* pp. 76, 77.

78. Klamkin, *Wood Carvings,* p. 26.

79. Horwitz, *The Bird, the Banner,* p. 84.

80. Jean Lipman, *American Folk Art* (Meriden, Conn.: Pantheon, 1948), p. 110.

81. Frederick Fried, *A Pictorial History of the Carousel* (New York: Bonanza Books, 1964), p. 165.

82. Patsy and Myron Orlofsky, *Quilts in America* (New York: McGraw-Hill, 1974), p. 218.

83. Jones, *Outward Signs,* p. 22.

84. Rhodes, *American Folk Art,* p. 50.

85. Ibid.

86. Ibid.

87. Jones, *Outward Signs,* pp. 47, 72.

88. Hornung, *Treasury of American Design,* p. 108.

89. Ibid.

90. Jean Lipman and Alice Winchester, *The Flowering of American Folk Art* (New York: The Viking Press in cooperation with the Whitney Museum of American Art, 1974), p. 93.

91. Ibid., p. 94.

92. Horwitz, *The Bird, the Banner,* p. 121.

93. Ibid., p. 86.

94. Trachtenberg, *Statue of Liberty,* p. 74.

95. Robert Bishop, *American Folk Sculpture* (New York: E.P. Dutton, 1974), p. 122.

96. Horwitz, *The Bird, the Banner,* p. 90.

97. Ibid., p. 107.

9. Artist unknown: *Liberty*. United States. Early nineteenth century. Oil on canvas, 29⅞″ x 20″. The girl, the eagle, the cup, and the flag are still present in this fresh variation on Savage's engraving, but here the eagle has changed the direction of his flight, Liberty wears a new costume, and now holds a flagpole. Her high-laced sandals echo the classical influence. (National Gallery of Art, Washington, D.C.; gift of Edgar William and Bernice Chrysler Garbisch)

10. Artist unknown: *Liberty in the Form of the Goddess of Youth Giving Support to the Bald Eagle*. United States. 1800–1830. Painting on velvet, 21½″ x 16⅜″. This interpretation of Savage's *Liberty* retains other symbols as well—the Liberty Cap on top of the flag and the broken scepter, the key to the Bastille, and the star of the Order of the Garter on the ground under her feet. This painting may have been created with the use of stencils, as the lines of Liberty's footwear suggest sandals. (Abby Aldrich Rockefeller Folk Art Center)

11. Attributed to Frederick Kemmelmeyer: *Emblem of the United States of America. Peace with All Nations Partiality to None.* Maryland. c. 1800. Oil on academy board, 19½″ x 21¼″. A female figure representing America (based on earlier representations of Britannia) sits on a globe showing North America, against which leans the Great Seal of the United States, and she holds a flag with twelve stars, which suggests a possible date of c. 1790, before Rhode Island joined the Union. In her right hand America holds the olive branch of peace, and the two ships in the background represent commerce and trade. In the foreground the palette and maulstick, lyre, books, and plow symbolize art, music, literature, and agriculture. The top of the monument is inscribed: *Sacred to the Memory of the Heroes of the American Revolution.* On the bottom is the inscription: *Beneath this Monument lies the Yoke of England and the Tyrant's Chain Buried Forever.* Photograph courtesy Museum of Art, Rhode Island School of Design, Providence, Rhode Island. (The Daphne Farago Americana Collection)

12. Montgomery C. Tiers: *Centennial Progress U.S.A. July 4, 1876.* New York. 1875. Oil on canvas, 68″ x 48¾″. A crowned Liberty, accompanied by all the presidents up to 1876, leads America to its destiny. All, including an American Indian, stand in a flag-draped boat decorated with carved eagles. A bolt of lightning and a kite, motifs associated with Benjamin Franklin, are seen in the sky together with an eagle. (Private collection)

13. Artist unknown (signed L.N.): *Liberty.* New York. 1864. Oil on canvas, 98″ x 60″. This powerful image of Liberty holds a tomahawk, and the Stars and Stripes is draped at her side with the laurel wreath of victory. (Collection of Allan L. Daniel)

14. Artist unknown: *Union Forever.* United States. c. 1906. Oil on canvas, 64″ x 40¼″. Liberty's Cap is decorated with stars and stripes, and the eagle is not only by her side but also serves as a finial on the flagpole. (Collection of Mary and John Fish)

15. Attributed to Betsey B. Lathrop: *Liberty in the Form of the Goddess of Youth Giving Support to the Bald Eagle*. United States. c. 1810. Watercolor on silk, 29″ x 29″. Enclosed in an oval of gold sequins sewn on the silk, this is an especially appealing interpretation of the engraving by E. Savage. The gold eagle and cup shine brightly, and the floral garland makes a delightful frame for it all. (Collection of Sybil and Arthur Kern)

16. Artist unknown: *America*. United States. 1815. Watercolor on paper, 13½″ x 11½″. A warlike eagle launches thunderbolts, symbolic of Zeus, toward a woman and a cowering lion symbolizing Britain. Liberty holds an American flag, and is protected by an American soldier. Her hair is held up by a band lettered *Liberty*. The flag of Britain lies rumpled on the ground in this watercolor of the War of 1812, when the British were driven away from America's shores. (New York State Historical Association)

17. Artist unknown: *Miss Liberty*. Probably New Jersey. 1810–1820. Watercolor, ink, and pinpricking on paper, 10¹/₁₆″ x 8¹/₁₆″. *Liberty and Independence* and *Ever Glorious Memory* are inscribed on the ground on which stands this chic, rosy-cheeked Liberty wearing clocked stockings and a bonnet tied with a streamered bow. She holds not only the Liberty Cap and pole but also an eagle-emblazoned flag. She is a delight. (Abby Aldrich Rockefeller Folk Art Center)

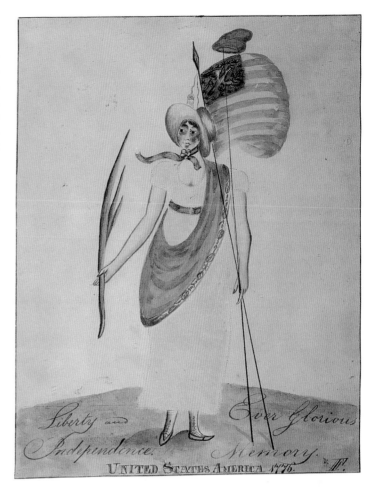

18. Artist unknown: *Emblem of Peace*. United States. 1823. Watercolor on paper, 14″ x 11¼″. A graceful palm, stylized cypress trees, and a strong, abstractly rendered landscape effectively set off the fragile, dark-haired Liberty with a fluttering eagle on her flag. (Collection of Agnes Halsey Jones and Louis C. Jones)

19. Artist unknown: *Memorial to General Washington.* United States. c. 1815. Watercolor on paper, 15¹³⁄₁₆" x 10⁵⁄₁₆". This long-legged Liberty—statuesque, beplumed, and brightly garbed—mourns the great Washington with her black Indian companion amid tropical foliage. (Philadelphia Museum of Art; gift of Edgar William and Bernice Chrysler Garbisch)

20. Artist unknown: *Columbia at Niagara Falls.* United States. 1810–1820. Watercolor on paper, 12" x 10". Flowers and trees represent the flora of the new country as the great Niagara, sacred to some Indian tribes in the East, thunders at the left. Columbia holds the Liberty Cap and pole, as well as a scrolled paper, probably intended to be the Declaration of Independence. (New York State Historical Association)

21. Artist unknown: *Columbia*. United States. Early nineteenth century. Watercolor on paper, 13″ x 11″. A blond-tressed Columbia with a laurel wreath in her hair and a bead necklace holds the flag and Liberty Cap on pole. (Collection of Dr. and Mrs. Ralph Katz)

22. Artist unknown: *Family Record*. Probably Massachusetts. 1829. Watercolor on paper, 16½″ x 21¼″. The names and vital statistics of the children of Samuel Bottomly and Sarah Livermore are inscribed within an elaborate neoclassical setting, flanked by two figures of Columbia holding American flags, shields, and Liberty Caps. An American eagle grasping crossed spears and floral swags surmounts the whole design. (Private collection)

23. Joe Miller: *Our Country Is Free*. Illinois. c. 1870. Water-color on paper, 14″ x 10″. A lovely dark-haired Liberty, veiled in delicate white lace, points to the furling flag and lettering in this work by an artist who sometimes signed his pieces *Linn Co., Oregon*. A tiny shield decorates the front of Liberty's tiara, and a poem, at bottom, continues this patriotic tribute. *Our Country Is Free* is clearly based on the small folio Currier and Ives color print *The Star Spangled Banner* #481, a widely circulated and often imitated series. (Collection of Merle H. Glick)

24. Peter Charlie Bochero: *Lady Liberty of 1953*. Leech-burg, Pennsylvania. 1953. Oil on canvas, 23″ x 28½″. Peter Charlie, a 1903 immigrant from Armenia, settled in Penn-sylvania, becoming a housepainter and jack-of-all-trades. He rented a garage behind a local hardware store and painted in secret, using whatever was handy—linoleum, canvas-weight fabric, and paper. Outer-space invaders, exhortations against false promises made by politicians and clergy, Eastern and Western religious symbols, mystical events, and idolatry of Abraham Lincoln characterized the sixty-nine personal visions found after the death of this "outsider-artist" revealing his tormented personality. Here a jet-flamed Lady Liberty spaceship flies across blue skies filled with personal messages, some recognizable—eyes, always a dominant feature in naive folk art; numbers and letters. (Collection of Herbert W. Hemphill, Jr.)

25. Michael Langenstein: *Swimmer of Liberty*. United States. 1976. Collage, 4″ x 6″. Surely there must have been more than one sweltering summer day when the Lady with the Lamp longingly imagined herself cooling off in New York Bay—as so wryly portrayed by Langenstein in this marvelous collage. Photograph courtesy the artist. (Collection of Elaine Steiner, Paris, France)

26. Gisela Fabian: *Liberty in the Palm of My Hand*. United States. c. 1984. Oil on canvas, 18″ x 24″. A flag-be-decked, blond-tressed mermaid rocks on a river buoy near Ellis Island, with its tree-dotted walkway, while she holds the Statue of Liberty in her hand. (Collection of Mr. and Mrs. James Grad)

27. William Hawkins: *The Statue of Liberty*. United States. 1984. Painting and assemblage with enamel, plastic, and metal, 48″ x 96″. Three ducks, a flag, a walking figure, a French airplane, a British ship, and houses complete this bright assemblage honoring the Statue of Liberty. (Collection of American Express)

28. Malcah Zeldis: *Mother of Exiles*. United States. 1985. Oil on Masonite, 30″ x 40″. A serene blue Mother of Exiles waves a welcome to arklike boats full of tourists approaching her green and flowered island. (Jay Johnson Gallery, New York City)

29. Kathy Jakobsen: *Statue of Liberty*. United States. 1985. Oil on canvas, 30″ x 40″. Flowerlike fireworks dazzle the skies over the Statue of Liberty amid schooners and ocean liners streaming by Ellis Island. Photograph courtesy Jay Johnson Gallery, New York City, and the artist. (Collection of Mr. and Mrs. Frank P. Wendt)

30. Artist unknown: *Indian Princess with Two Pilgrims*. United States. c. 1750. Needlework, 10¾" x 13¾". Two pilgrims and the Indian Princess are surrounded by animals, birds, strawberries—a popular New England motif—flowers, and fruit trees, with a house in the background. Scallops edge the inner frame of this wool-and-silk-on-linen embroidery incorporating stem, buttonhole, bullion, Rumanian couching, surface satin, and cross-stitches. (The Metropolitan Museum of Art; gift of Screven Lorillard, 1953)

31. Artist unknown: *Liberty and Washington Memorial*. Origin unknown. 1805–1810. Needlework picture, 15" x 19". This splendid memorial to Washington was probably based on the central cartouche of a printed kerchief or on the print that inspired the kerchief. Motifs from printed memorials—George Washington, Benjamin Franklin, and a figure dressed as a blonde Indian Princess gazing at a Grecian-garbed Goddess of Liberty holding the Liberty Cap on pole—simultaneously satisfied patriotic fervor and a taste for neoclassisicm. The setting sun and the departing boat signify the end of life: the death of George Washington. (Private collection)

32. Probably made by Joanna Henrietta Harsen: *Indian Princess with American Flag and Anchor.* United States. Early nineteenth century. Needlework, 7″ x 4½″. An Indian Princess with braided hair holds the American flag while leaning on an anchor, the symbol of hope, in this crudely embroidered muslin. (Museum of the City of New York; gift of Mrs. R. N. Willcox)

33. Artist unknown: *Liberty in the Form of the Goddess of Youth Giving Support to the Bald Eagle in Front of the Trenton Arches.* New Jersey or New York. c. 1800. Needlework, 26¾″ x 28⅜″. Silk threads, watercolor, sequins, and mica on silk depict the Goddess of Liberty posed before the Trenton Arches, erected to honor George Washington en route to take his oath as the first president of the United States. The goddess's head, neck, arms, chest, feet, and goblet, as well as the sky, the eagle's tongue, the view of Trenton, and the blue field of the flag are painted, while remaining sections are sewn with French knot, flat, bullion, seed, and satin stitchery. (The Daughters of the American Revolution Museum, Washington, D.C.)

34. Cynthia Bushwell Wilcox: *Memorial to Washington.* Probably Middletown, Connecticut. 1804. Needlework, paint and silk thread on silk, 17½″ x 14″. This memorial to the first president, painted on silk and stitched with silk thread, shows a dark-ringleted Liberty offering a cup to the American eagle. (Private collection)

35. Artist unknown: *Goddess of Liberty*. United States. c. 1860. Copper weathervane, 27″ x 18½″ x 2″. This plump but endearing representation of the Goddess of Liberty may be nearly identical to one manufactured by the Fiske Company and advertised in its 1893 catalogue, where it was available in a 24-inch or a 36-inch size. The Fiske vane, like the one illustrated here, had punched stars on the flag, on the band of the Liberty Cap, and on the draped sash over the bosom. (Private collection)

36. Artist unknown: *Goddess of Liberty*. United States. c. 1870. Weathervane, gilded and painted copper, H. 35¼″. A red, white, and blue flag waves gaily as Liberty, white-sashed and crowned with the Liberty Cap, statuesquely performs her duty. (Private collection)

37. Artist unknown: *Goddess of Liberty*. New England. Late nineteenth century. Weathervane, molded and gilded copper and cast zinc, 43″ x 38″. Originally gilded, this Goddess of Liberty vane has a molded and flattened form. Her unusual short cloak catches the wind over her shoulders. She grasps the American flag with punched five-point stars while holding the fasces and the traditional ax. Fasces or bundles of rods were originally carried before magistrates in ancient Rome as an emblem of authority. (Private collection)

38. Artist unknown: *Columbia*. Waltham, Massachusetts. c. 1865. Copper weathervane, 38″ x 27″ x 2″. This elegant Columbia vane was saved from a burning schoolhouse and found in Ogunquit, Maine. The vane was probably made by Cushing and White, Waltham, Massachusetts. (Collection of William L. Harrington)

39. Henry Leach: *Columbia*. United States. c. 1868. Weathervane, painted and gilded wood, H. 46″. The folded bodice of Columbia's togalike garment is held by two rosettes as she points the direction of the wind. Found in the Virgin Islands, this handsome vane was first thought to be a ship's figurehead, and it served as the pattern for a weathervane made by Cushing and White of Waltham, Massachusetts. (The Shelburne Museum, Shelburne, Vermont)

40. J.L. Mott Iron Works: *Statue of Liberty.* New York and Chicago. c. 1886. Weathervane, hammered copper with original parcel gilding, 53″ x 54″ x 5″. Almost five feet high, this weathervane is the closest in appearance of known existing vanes to the Statue of Liberty. (Private collection)

41. James Leonard: *The Statue of Liberty Being Repaired.* New Jersey. 1984. Whirligig weathervane, copper with liver of sulfate markings, 37″ x 10¾″ x 27¾″. American folk artists are still fascinated with the windtoy and still incorporate patriotic symbols in their designs. The restoration of the Statue of Liberty for the Centennial celebrations inspired this whirligig, complete with workers busily making her beautiful for her 100th birthday party. (Collection of Kathy Willner)

42. Artist unknown: *Goddess of Liberty*. Origin unknown. 1850–1860. Ship figurehead, carved and painted wood, 70″ x 19″ x 22½″. Figureheads, wooden carvings on the prow, were used as talismans to get ships safely into port. Following the American Revolution, a wide variety of patriotic symbols were adapted by figurehead carvers—the eagle, the early patriots, and also Miss Liberty, who symbolized not only a free nation but also that the sailing fleet of the United States believed in free trade and sailors' rights. This Goddess of Liberty, holding a flaming torch, is dressed in a blue classical costume. (State Street Bank Corporate Art Collection, Boston, Massachusetts)

43. Samuel Robb Studio: *Indian Princess*. New York. 1875–1900. Cigar-store figure, carved and painted wood, H. 69″. The Indians, the first Americans to cultivate and smoke tobacco, introduced it to sixteenth-century explorers and adventurers from Portugal, Spain, and England. At first the foreigners used tobacco medicinally—to cure cancer, ironically—before the vogue of smoking swept Europe. Tobacco was associated with the New World, as was the Indian Princess, the second symbol of America used in the Old World. These carvings were made from various woods and vividly painted, then coated for protection against the elements with a hole drilled in the head so that linseed oil could be added for preservation. American cigar-store figures were generally of two types: the smaller countertop or store window version, carved on a base, and the larger street carving, sometimes set on rollers for easy mobility. Originally, the Indians were carved by a single artist, but the demand so increased with the growth of the young country that soon several carvers were working in one shop. The birth of mail-order catalogues substantially heightened the demand, and in response, white-metal examples were cast—signaling the death of this folk-art "industry." (Museum of American Folk Art, New York City; gift of Mrs. Gertrude Schweitzer)

44. William Frederick White: *Liberty in the Form of the Goddess of Youth Giving Support to the Bald Eagle*. Ashburnham, Massachusetts. c. 1860. Trade sign, oil on canvas, 47½″ x 61″ x 46″. This scrolled canvas sign, mounted on a double layer of pine, belonged to and advertised a professional ornamental painter, William Frederick White, of Ashburnham. Its motif of a girl feeding an eagle shows the deep roots Savage's *Liberty* had taken in the psyche of America. (Morgan B. Brainard Collection, The Connecticut Historical Society, Hartford, Connecticut)

45. Artist unknown: *Justice of the Peace.* Appleton, Ohio. c. 1880. Trade sign, painted wood, 21″ x 30½″ x 2″. A girlish Miss Liberty gives sustenance to the American eagle while she holds the sword and the scales of justice. The sculptures are supported by a wooden triangle that topped a justice of the peace office in Appleton, Ohio. The bright color of Liberty's red dress, the light and dark of the eagle feathers, and the touches of gold on the sword and scales make this a striking update of Savage's engraving. (New York State Historical Association)

46. Artist unknown: *Columbia.* United States. c. 1858. Deck figure, painted wood, 66½″ x 16½″ x 13″. This Columbia, an inventive combination of the name of America's discoverer, Christopher Columbus, with a classical deity, once stood before the pilothouse of a Great Lakes steamer. A shield is beside her, and she holds a golden ball symbolizing the earth in her left hand. (New York State Historical Association)

47. Artist unknown: *Miss Liberty*. Tilton, New Hampshire. 1850–1860. Sculpture, painted wood, H. 25¾″. Many versions of Liberty show her as the defender of America, and this daunting figure from a boathouse in Tuftonborough, New Hampshire, with her sword and rippling flag, unmistakably conveys her bold intentions. (The Barenholtz Collection)

48. Artist unknown: *Columbia*. United States. 1875-1900. Sculpture, painted wood, 78″ x 21″ x 21½″. The source for this architectural decoration or parade figure may have been a zinc sculpture by M. J. Seeling and Company of Williamsburg, Virginia, sold under William Demuth's name. Carved from one piece of pine, this large Liberty has a hole in the top of her head in which oil can be placed to preserve the wood. (Abby Aldrich Rockefeller Folk Art Center)

49. Artist unknown: *Liberty with Flag.* © 1980 with base. Origin unknown. Late nineteenth century. Sculpture, H. 15″. Carved from one piece of wood, Liberty wears the cap and salutes the flag with her left hand, while holding the flagpole with its flag furling around the shield-decorated bodice of her dress. The folds of the flag make a pleasing design element, continuing into the drape of her gown. (Barbara Johnson Collection)

50. Artist unknown: *Liberty.* Coastal Massachusetts. 1790–1810. Sculpture, painted white pine, H. 53⁷/₁₆″. A demure yet bare-breasted, barefoot Liberty holds the Liberty Cap and pole and a wreath of flowers and leaves. In this sculpture the Liberty Cap and pole are replacements, and the wreath has been restored. (Museum of Fine Arts, Boston; H. E. Bolles Fund)

51. Artist unknown: *Birth of a Nation.* © 1973.
New York. 1848. Cast-iron stove figure, H. 48″.
Ferromania echoed the rapid growth of the iron
industry in the United States and reflected the
ingenuity of Americans who cast a wide variety of
articles, for use in homes, gardens, stores, summer
resorts, and country retreats. Sometimes painted,
stove figures were as utilitarian as they were beautiful, for attached to a boxlike stove, they served as
heat radiators. (Barbara Johnson Collection)

52. Artist unknown: *Liberty*. Manufactured by W.H. Mullins Company, Salem, Ohio. c. 1880. Metal sculpture, H. 20″. This beautiful crowned head of Liberty is all that has survived from a Soldiers' Monument in Allentown, Pennsylvania. Photograph courtesy G. William Holland. (Private collection)

53. Artist unknown: *Goddess of Liberty Andirons*. United States. Nineteenth century. Cast-iron andirons, 18″ x 4″. These finely cast andirons feature beautifully draped Liberty figures holding flaming torches. Photograph courtesy Joan Rafferty. (American Primitive Gallery, New York City)

54. Elidoro Parete: *Liberty (United States of America)*. Anawalt, West Virginia. c. 1863. Sculpture, painted wood, H. 32¼". Italian religious processional or cathedral art may have inspired an Italian immigrant to create this doll-like seated Liberty. A dog holding a book and a flower-strewn pedestal are charming additions to this diademed Liberty. (The Shelburne Museum)

56. Artist unknown: *Columbia*. Pennsylvania. Nineteenth century. Sculpture, gilded wood, H. 17½″. The unknown carver of this small Liberty may have been influenced by the metal sculptures that were popular as building finials, recess decorations, and lawn ornaments for patriotic and fraternal organizations. It especially recalls the work of William Demuth, as the wood is carved to resemble cast iron. (Collection of Allen E. and Ellen Cober)

55. Artist unknown: *Liberty*. United States. Late nineteenth century. Sculpture, painted wood, 17″ to top of flagstaff, 13″ to top of figure. A dainty laced shoe peeks out from the décolleté blue robe of this delightful Liberty, holding a sword and flag. (Collection of Dr. and Mrs. Ralph Katz)

57. Artist unknown: *The Statue of Liberty*. Argo's Corner, Delaware. c. 1900. Wood and wrought iron, 18½″ x 6″. An unknown primitive artist designed this gatepost finial using the natural grain of the pine to emphasize the lines of the robe and of the upthrust arm, where traces of mustard yellow and brown paint remain. Black paint is visible on the hair and on the Declaration of Independence tablet under the arm. Although missing her torch, this quaint Statue of Liberty still retains her crown of nine rays made of old, flattened nails. Photograph courtesy Jeff Li. (Collection of Peggy W. Lancaster)

58. Artist unknown: *Liberty*. Connecticut. Early twentieth century. Sculpture, carved and painted wood, H. 82″. This ingenuous Liberty, made from a thick post, has a heart-shaped shield inscribed *Liberty*, holds a sword, and has a primitive cannon by her side. A jagged crown caps her smiling face. (The Hall Collection of American Folk Art and Isolate Art)

59. Isaac Bindman: *The Liberty Money Box*. Corona, New York. c. 1880. Carved and applied wood, 14″ x 4½″. After its demonstration at the 1876 Philadelphia Centennial, jigsaw fever swept the country, aided by the power of treadle machines. Men, women, and children alike learned this scrollsawing art and earned money by cutting and selling household ornaments. This money box is a rare survivor of late nineteenth-century jigsawed "gingerbread" art and was used to collect donations for the construction of the base for the Statue of Liberty on Bedloe's Island. (Moquin House Antiques)

60. Artist unknown: *Liberty*. Origin unknown. Early twentieth century. Sculpture, gilded wood, 38″ x 14″. The folk artist's use of found materials is embodied in this blue-eyed Statue of Liberty, with golden curls made of wood shavings. Its gold paint symbolizes the richness of the new country. (Private collection)

61. Artist unknown: *Statue of Liberty.* New Jersey. c. 1940. Sculpture, 40″ x 8½″ x 8½″. This twentieth-century Liberty, found in northern New Jersey, is constructed of wood, plaster, bronze paint, and colored glass shards. A working light bulb simulates the real torch. (Collection of Jacqueline Donegan)

62. Karl Wittman: *Statue of Liberty.* United States. 1955–1960. Sculpture, stained oak and basswood in three sections, H. 96″. A twentieth-century immigrant, in gratitude for his escape from East Germany, created this Statue of Liberty and gave it to the people of his first home in the United States, Cattaraugus, New York. (Cattaraugus Area Historical Society)

63. Leslie J. Payne: *New York Lady*. Virginia. 1975. Sculpture, painted tin, hair, jewelry, and wood, 25″ x 14″ x 7″. Large mascaraed eyes, a six-rayed crown, dangling earrings, and a buttoned dress give this "lady" a saucy look. Photograph courtesy W. D. Pieri III. (Collection of Martin and Enid Packard)

64. Edward Ambrose: *Miss Liberty*. Virginia. 1975. Sculpture, painted wood, H. 18″. A gleeful Liberty holds a sword in her right hand and shield of stars and stripes in her left , a motif repeated in the toga draped over her T-shirt. Her impudent face and brilliantly painted toenails in classical sandals add whimsy to this twentieth-century "mighty woman." (Collection of Elinor Lander Horwitz)

65. Robert Ramsour: Detail of *Statue of Liberty*. Denver, Colorado. 1984. Sculpture, sheet metal, H. 131″. This striking version of Liberty was made by a plumbing and heating contractor, using sheet metal and spare parts, to encourage local students to donate funds for the refurbishing of the Statue of Liberty. (Collection of Robert Ramsour)

66. Artist unknown: *Miss America on a Tightrope*. United States. 1835–1850. Print from wood block, 17½″ x 32″. Here called Miss America, tightrope-walking Liberty is dressed in stars and stripes. The ribbon sash at her waist, her coiffure, and the Grecian urn filled with stylized foliage reflect the popular classical influences of the time. The original wood block was probably used to print eye-catching broadsides announcing the arrival of a traveling circus and was probably colored in red, white and blue. The printing block has survived in fine condition only because it was used as the back of a box for a ship model of the period, to which it is still attached. (New York State Historical Association)

68. Artist unknown: Centennial Coverlet inscribed *Hail Columbia*. United States. 1886. Woven wool and cotton coverlet, 82″ x 82″. Bands of different colors add zest to a rare coverlet inspired by the Centennial celebrations of 1876. Twin figures of Liberty at left and right hold rippling flags, while eagles in the four corners clasp in their beaks banners inscribed *Hail Columbia*. Photograph courtesy Mark Diehl. (Private collection)

67. Artist unknown: *Apotheosis of George Washington and Benjamin Franklin*. England. c. 1800. Copperplate-printed cotton and linen, 41″ x 30″. This English toile was printed in several colors for export to America. It was extremely popular because it featured many American symbols—George Washington, Benjamin Franklin, Liberty with her pole and cap, the "Liberty Tree," the Plumed Goddess, the black American Indian, the flag with rattlesnake, design and small angels holding a map showing the thirteen Colonies. (Museum of Fine Arts, Boston; gift of Miss Mary E. G. Norcross)

69. J. Van Ness: Detail of a coverlet inscribed *Liberty*. Palmyra, New York. 1849. Woven wool and cotton, dimensions of complete coverlet: 95″ x 82″. Portraits of Miss Liberty, framed by laurel branches and paired American flags are some of the motifs in the central medallion of this unusual coverlet. (New York State Historical Association)

70. Artist unknown: *Anna Yates Cake Board*. Schenectady, New York. Eighteenth century. Cake board, black walnut, 7⅜″ x 13½″. An elaborately dressed Indian Princess with feathered headdress, with a handsome rose at the left and a bird on a spray of leaves at the right, holds a parrot in this rare, two-sided, carved cake board from the Yates family of Schenectady, New York. (Private collection)

71. Henry Cox: *Washington Memorial Cake Board*. United States. Third quarter of nineteenth century. Cake board, 15″ x 25½″. This elliptical mold shows a memorial to Washington flanked by two female figures. The figure on the right nourishes a hovering eagle in the familiar pose of the E. Savage engraving (fig. 4), while the other holds a Liberty Cap on pole. The American shield and two flags with another cap and pole are carved on the right, and an Indian brave stands majestically at the left. (New York State Historical Association)

72. Artist unknown: *Tin Cookie Cutter*. Pennsylvania. Late nineteenth or early twentieth century. 4¼″ x 3⁷⁄₁₆″. The design of this rare piece is based on the Coronet type of Liberty head, as opposed to the earlier Liberty Cap or turban type that appeared on various American coins. It has been designed facing to the right so that a cookie made with it would have the Liberty head facing left, as in the coins. This cutter is soldered all around the rim, an aid in dating, for the earliest cutters were spot soldered. Photograph courtesy Jeff Li. (Collection of Peggy W. Lancaster)

73. Artist unknown: *Mount Airy Fire Company Hat.* The Philadelphia Contributionship. c. 1840. 6″ x 11¾″ x 12¾″. From the water-bucket brigade to twentieth-century technology, fire-fighting paraphernalia has given us many beautifully decorated items based on historical, classical, contemporary, and even patriotic figures. This hand-painted and decorated stovepipe hat, worn mainly for dress parades, features Liberty draped in the Stars and Stripes, and she holds a shield and the Liberty Cap and pole. (Collection of The Philadelphia Contributionship)

74. Artist unknown: *Hebe Feeding Zeus.* United States. c. 1832. Fire-engine panel, oil on wood, 29¾″ x 17¼″. Although fire-fighting equipment was utilitarian, it was often embellished with carved or elaborately painted symbolic decorations. This panel from a fire engine shows Hebe feeding Zeus, the classical theme that inspired the Savage engraving. (The Cigna Museum and Art Collection, Philadelphia, Pennsylvania)

75. Artist unknown: *Washington Memorial*. Origin unknown. 1815–1820. Cut-paper picture, 14⅝″ x 12¼″. This *Scherenschnitte* or scissors-cut Liberty, silhouetted against a piece of mirror glass, offers support to the Bald Eagle while she holds the scales and tramples the British crown underfoot. Virtue or Truth reads a book labeled *Truth* while a globe, scrolls, and a quiver signify that concepts of justice, equality, and liberty will be proclaimed by paper if possible; or if necessary, asserted by force. A large, weeping willow droops over the stepped monument to George Washington, with flowers at its base, while a bugle, flag, drum, and sword recall his life. (The Daughters of the American Revolution Museum)

76. Artist unknown: *Liberty of the Seas.* © 1982. United States. 1847. Scrimshaw, sperm whale's tooth, 6″ x 2″. Liberty, with the Indian Princess's face, is depicted with a mermaid's tail, part of seafaring folklore still prevalent at the time. A Liberty Cap appears overhead. Liberty is accompanied by an American Indian, an eagle with a mermaid's tail, and a tiger clawing a tree, reminiscent of the Indian Queen period. (Barbara Johnson Collection)

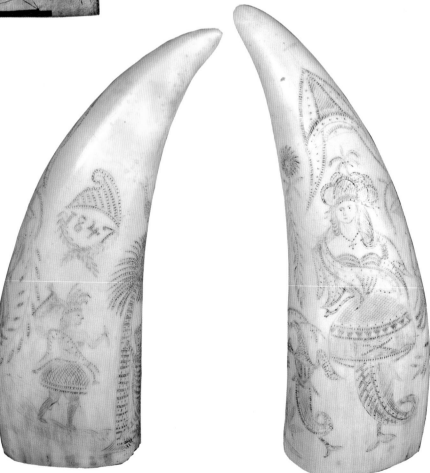

77. Artist unknown: *Columbia*. Probably New England. 1850–1870. Scrimshaw, H. 5″. Scrimshaw was a decorative art created by sailors on New England whaling ships during their free time on the long voyages. Most scrimshaw is incised and colored, so this Columbia carved in bold relief is unusual. Jackknives, saws, gimlets for drilling holes, files, grindstones, sailmaker's needles for incising, and ink and wood ashes for finishing were among these artists' tools. (Collection of Dr. Angelo J. De Falco)

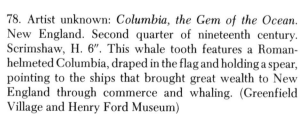

78. Artist unknown: *Columbia, the Gem of the Ocean*. New England. Second quarter of nineteenth century. Scrimshaw, H. 6″. This whale tooth features a Roman-helmeted Columbia, draped in the flag and holding a spear, pointing to the ships that brought great wealth to New England through commerce and whaling. (Greenfield Village and Henry Ford Museum)

79. Artist unknown: *Columbia with Liberty Cap Facing Left*. Union Glass Works, Kensington, Philadelphia, Pennsylvania. c. 1820. Blown, three-mold flask in aquamarine glass, H. 7⁵⁄₁₆". An American eagle is on the opposite side of this flask. (The Corning Museum of Glass, Corning, New York)

80. Artist unknown: *Doll*. Probably New York. c. 1893. Muslin stuffed with cotton and sawdust and with hand-painted face, 19½" x 8" x 3¾". This charming doll was probably inspired by the Columbia dolls made by the Adams Sisters that won an award at the World's Columbian Exposition held in Chicago, Illinois, in 1893. (Collection of Mrs. Charlotte Moore)

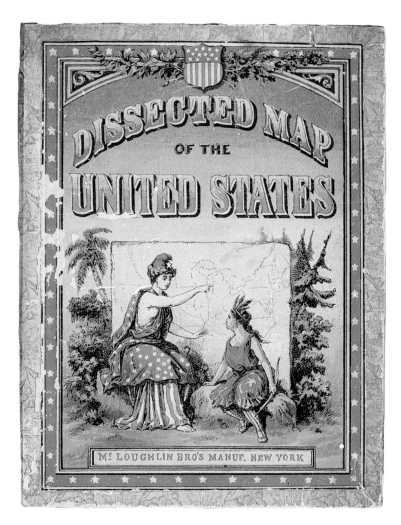

81. Artist unknown: *Dissected Map of the United States.* Labeled: McLoughlin Bros. Manuf. New York. 1870–1890. Game, 9¾″ x 7½″. Flag-draped, Liberty-Capped Liberty explains to the Indian Princess the map of the United States of America. (Private collection)

82. Artist unknown: *Liberty and Flag.* Probably New England. Late nineteenth or early twentieth century. Kaleidoscope, 7″ x 2″. This hand-painted red, white, blue, and gold kaleidoscope shows a naïvely stylish Liberty, draped in the stripes of a swirling flag, while the whole composition is spattered with gold stars. (Marna Anderson Gallery, New York City)

83. Artist unknown: *Miss Liberty*. United States. Twentieth century. Ice-cream mold, 5¾″ x 3″ x 2¼″. S and Co., No. 559. The rage for colored, molded ice cream flourished at the turn of the century and well into the twentieth. Pewter molds were made in such shapes as flowers, fruit, animals, sports, as well as special shapes for Christmas, Easter, and Valentine's Day; and such patriotic symbols as eagles, shields, flags, George Washington, and even Miss Liberty. (Private collection)

84. Artist unknown: *Sweet Liberty*. United States. c. 1890. Cigar-box label, 5″ x 9″. "Sweet Liberty" sits with the shield and holds the American flag and a palm branch, amid flowers and palms. Indian children brandishing tobacco leaves accompany her in this seaside scene with cargo ships and a lighthouse. The feathered clothing and the bow and arrows of the Indian children recall the first image of America, one still familiar and recognizable. (Private collection)

85. The Republican Publishing Company: *The Columbia Carriage Company*. Hamilton, Ohio. 1903. Trademark, 5″ x 6¾″. Americans of all levels of education, sophistication, and wealth loved their land and venerated the symbols of their nationhood, displaying them everywhere, often in advertising. This carriage-company trademark in the then-fashionable Art Nouveau style shows Columbia wearing the Liberty Cap and holding the shield and laurel wreath. (The Museums at Stony Brook, New York, Carriage Reference Library)

86. George William Sotter: *New Jersey State Seal*. State House Annex, Trenton, New Jersey. 1929. Stained-glass window, 36″ x 60″. Floral borders enclose the central design in this handsome stained-glass panel, showing Liberty, holding a Liberty Cap and pole, and Prosperity, holding a cornucopia filled with fruit, in this version of the New Jersey State Seal. (New Jersey State Museum, Trenton, New Jersey)

87. C. B. Spies: *Liberty*. United States. 1918. Oil on canvas, 45″ x 30″. American artists are still inspired by popular prints, as in this painting based on a litho poster *U.S.A. Bonds*, advertising the Third Liberty Loan Campaign, the Boy Scouts of America, and Weapons for Liberty. This painting is inscribed: *From Leyendecker by C. B. Spies 1918.* (Georgia Museum of Art, The University of Georgia, Athens, Georgia)

88. John Heinly: *Ducking the Tomatoes*. Washington, D.C. 1975. Ink drawing. Patriotism was often considered a dirty word in the 1960s and 1970s, as is vividly shown in this satirical drawing by cartoonist and illustrator John Heinly. (Collection of Elinor Lander Horwitz)

89. Artist unknown: *Pinup Girl as Liberty.* United States. c. 1940. 6″ x 4½″. This pinup bathing beauty with beach umbrella of the 1940s Betty Grable era is scantily clad in a two-piece Stars-and-Stripes bathing suit. (Collection of Curtis F. Brown)

90. Artist unknown: *Pop Art Night-Light of Torch and Hand of the Statue of Liberty.* United States. c. 1970. H. 8½″. Two American totems—the ice-cream cone and the Statue of Liberty—are combined in this plastic night-light. It is the wry genius of true kitsch that paints Liberty's fingernails a bright pink. (Collection of Curtis F. Brown)

91. Hebrew Publishing Company, New York: *New Year's Greeting Card*. c. 1915. 4¹⁄₁₆″ x 3⅜″. The American bald eagle hovers protectively over Liberty, dressed in the Stars and Stripes, as she unlocks the gates to the New World for a family of immigrants. Hebrew inscriptions on the card welcome the New Year and state: *Matron American Opens the Gates of a Just Nation*. (National Museum of American Jewish History, Washington, D.C.; gift of Barbara Kirshenblatt-Gimblett)

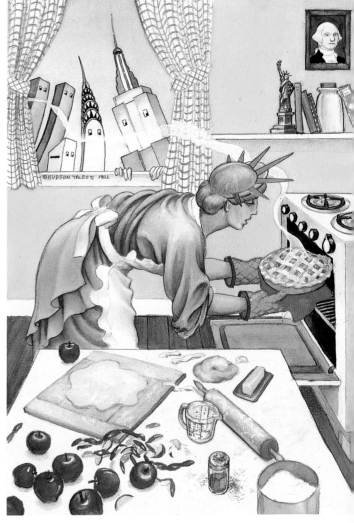

92. Hudson Talbott for Ruby Street, Inc.: *Apple Pie*. United States. 1982. Greeting card, 7⅛″ x 5⅛″. A conscientious housewife in white ruffled apron, the Statue of Liberty carefully removes a juicy pie from her oven, while being avidly watched by New York skyscrapers, hungry for "mom's apple pie." George Washington's portrait properly decorates the cheery kitchen with gingham curtains, and a Statue of Liberty souvenir serves as a bookend. (Collection of Hudson Talbott)

93. Hudson Talbott for Bloomingdale's: *American Gothic Christmas*. United States. 1982. Greeting card, 6½″ x 5¾″. Yet once again Grant Wood's long-suffering *American Gothic* has inspired a delightful spoof—this time pairing the Statue of Liberty and Uncle Sam. (Collection of Hudson Talbott)

94. José Balcells Pallares: *Semi-sweet Chocolate Statue of Liberty*. Barcelona, Spain. 1984. Chocolate, H. 102″. Here is the Statue of Liberty immortalized in 229 pounds of chocolate. José Balcells Pallares and his assistant, Xavier Salvat, created this extraordinary piece in three days. (© James L. Stanfield, National Geographic Society)

95. Michael Langenstein: *American Liberty*. New York. 1984. Computer graphics, created on a Dicomed D38. These stunning images of Liberty's head eloquently testify to the continuing artistic inspiration to be found in America's proudest symbol. (Collection of the artist)